RADIO OPERATOR
ON THE
EASTERN FRONT

RADIO OPERATOR ON THE EASTERN FRONT

An Illustrated Memoir, 1940–1949

Erhard Steiniger

Foreword by

Anthony Tucker-Jones

Translated by

Geoffrey Brooks

GREENHILL BOOKS

Radio Operator on the Eastern Front
This English-language edition
first published in 2020 by
Greenhill Books,
c/o Pen & Sword Books Ltd,
47 Church Street, Barnsley,
S. Yorkshire, S70 2AS

www.greenhillbooks.com
contact@greenhillbooks.com

ISBN: 978-1-78438-618-4

Publishing History
First published in Germany in 2019 as
Als Funker an den Brennpunkten der Front
by Verlagshaus Würzburg GmbH & Co. KG.
Flechsig Verlag, Beethovenstraße 5 B
D-97080 Würzburg

This is the first English-language edition
and includes a new foreword by Anthony Tucker-Jones

CIP data records for this title are available from the British Library

Designed and typeset by Donald Sommerville

Printed and bound in the UK by TJ Books Limited, Padstow

Typeset in 12/15.5 pt Minion Pro

Contents

Translator's Note

Where a person's German rank is mentioned in the original text, I have retained this in the translation for the sake of consistency. The British equivalents of German ranks up to the level of *Oberst* are as follows:

Gefreiter	Trained private soldier
Obergefreiter	Lance-corporal, but without NCO status
Unteroffizier	Corporal (trained NCO)
Unterfeldwebel	Lance-Sergeant
Feldwebel	Sergeant
Oberfeldwebel	Staff Sergeant
Stabsfeldwebel	Warrant Officer Class II
Hauptfeldwebel	Warrant Officer Class I
Leutnant	Second Lieutenant
Oberleutnant	Lieutenant
Hauptmann	Captain
Major	Major
Oberstleutnant	Lieutenant-Colonel
Oberst	Colonel

Geographical Names

Similarly I have generally retained German place names to preserve the spirit of the original text, though postwar political changes have made many of these outdated. The list overleaf includes many of these names with their modern equivalents.

Arensburg	Kuressaare	Mitau	Jelgava
Asch	Aš	Moon	Muhu
Beraun	Beroun	Neidenburg	Nidzica
Bilin	Bílina	Nidden	Nida
Birsen	Běrzpils	Ösel	Saaremaa
Braunsberg	Braniewo	Pardubitz	Pardubice
Bruch	Lom	Pogegen	Pagėgai
Brüx	Most	Preschen	Břešťany
Cranz	Zelenogradsk	Reval	Tallinn
Dagö	Hilumaa	Riesengebirge	Krkonoše
Danzig	Gdansk	Rössel	Reszel
Düna	Daugava	Schaulen	Šiauliai
Dux	Duchov	Schillen	Zilino
Ebenrode	Nesterov	Schweidnitz	Świdnica
Elbing	Elbląg	Segewold	Sigulda
Ermland	Warmia	Stalinsk	Novekuznetsk
Fellin	Viljandi	Striegau	Strzegom
Freiburg (Silesia)	Świebodzice	Sworbe	Sõrve
Gotenhafen	Gdynia	Teplitz-Schönau	Teplice-Šanov
Gross-Scharlack	Nakhimovo	Tilsit	Sovetsk
Gumbinnen	Gusev	Trakehnen	Yasnaya Polyana
Heydekrug	Šilutė		
Insterburg	Chernyakhovsk	Trautenau	Trutnov
Komorn	Komárno	Tuckum	Tukums
Königgratz	Hradec Králové	Wainoden	Vaiņode
Königsberg	Kaliningrad	Waldenburg (Silesia)	Wałbrzych
Korschen	Korsze		
Labiau	Polessk	Walk	Valga
Langugest	Jenišův Újezd	Wannow	Vaňov
Leitomischl	Litomyšl	Weckelsdorf	Teplice nad Metují
Libau	Liepāja		
Litzmannstadt	Łódź	Wesenberg	Rakvere
Memel (city/district)	Klaipėda	Wolmar	Valmiera
Memel (river)	Neman	Zoppot	Sopot

Foreword

I HAVE LONG BEEN A STUDENT of the Second World War's Eastern Front, a simply vast conflict that is largely neglected in the West. Only in recent years has a growing body of German and Russian memoirs, translated into English, made it much more accessible to a wider audience. Erhard Steiniger's wartime biography is the sort of volume that is the lifeblood of a historian, because it shows exactly what it was like to fight at grass-roots level. Steiniger saw action on the northern sector which, apart from the fighting for Leningrad, tends to be overshadowed by the combat to the south, especially the bitter battles for the control of Moscow and Ukraine. It was nonetheless the scene of a series of ferocious and brutal campaigns. In many ways his experiences are similar to those of Guy Sajer, who wrote that classic Eastern Front first-hand account *The Forgotten Soldier.*

Steiniger served as a signaller, or radio man, with the 151st Infantry Regiment, part of the 61st East Prussian Infantry Division throughout the war. He saw action in Lithuania, Latvia, Estonia, Russia and then Latvia again. Being a signaller hardly seemed a glamorous job, but at least it offered the prospect of regularly being protected within the confines of a headquarters bunker. However, in reality, trudging along with the infantry and burdened down with their radio equipment, signallers presented ideal targets for snipers. Steiniger and his platoon were responsible for keeping highly dispersed companies and battalions in communication, as well as calling down artillery fire and summoning Stuka dive bombers. This was a key job, especially as the war progressed and the battlefield became increasingly confused.

His experiences were no different to the hundreds of thousands of others who fought in Russia, but he was fortunate. He survived to tell his tale, despite the wholesale destruction of his division and his subsequent incarceration in Stalin's Gulag for four long years. Steiniger began writing his autobiography for the benefit of his family, very modestly stating 'I have no great adventures to recount, nor even really unusual experiences . . .' He does himself a great disservice in light of what he went through. Notably though, he does not shy away from describing the full horrors of war and the brutally obscene evisceration of soldiers on both sides.

Steiniger, like Sajer, was initially not a German citizen, rather *Volksdeutsche*, part of the Germanic diaspora that Adolf Hitler sought to reclaim for the Third Reich. He was born a Sudeten German and grew up as one of a persecuted minority in the new state of Czechoslovakia. This had been created from the ashes of the Austro-Hungarian Empire in the wake of the First World War. It was an unwieldy patchwork quilt of at least half a dozen different nationalities, all of whom, except the Czechs, struggled to find a true sense of national identity within Czechoslovakia.

Not surprisingly the Sudeten Germans were heartened when Hitler came to power in 1933 and began to call for the return of the *Volksdeutsche* to the Fatherland. Steiniger recalled 'Very nearly all of us Germans living on the Czech side of the Saxon border were thrilled by the news.' In response the Czech government banned Hitler's Nazi Party, but grudgingly tolerated the burgeoning Sudeten German Party. The Sudeten Germans welcomed Hitler when he took possession of the Sudetenland five years later. 'Sunday 10 October 1938 was the day of our liberation,' said Steiniger with evident pride.

In 1940, thanks to his German origins, Steiniger was conscripted into the German Army. He set off from his home in Langugest for Beraun via Prague, where he was to join the 21st Infantry Signals Reserve Company. Sent to occupied Brittany, he was assigned to the signals platoon of the 151st Infantry Regiment. That summer the Red Army, which was already occupying eastern Poland thanks to the Molotov–Ribbentrop Pact, invaded Estonia, Latvia and Lithuania. Steiniger's fate was to serve there as a frontline radio operator.

By early 1941 he and his regiment were in East Prussia ready for the invasion of the Soviet Union. They moved to the city of Memel, the capital of the *Volksdeutsche* region known as the *Memelland*, taken from Lithuania only two years earlier. Major General Siegefried Haenicke and the men of his 61st Infantry Division, part of the German Eighteenth Army, braced themselves for the coming battle. Steiniger's regiment was commanded by Colonel Walter Melzer.

'On 22 June 1941 at 0315 hrs our artillery opened fire. The grey dawn thundered with shellfire,' noted Steiniger. 'Fear overcame me, I sweated, my stomach revolted.' This bombardment heralded Operation Barbarossa, Hitler's titanic assault on Joseph Stalin's totalitarian Soviet Union. Steiniger would soon learn to hate his heavy radio, which only had a range of 3 km unless it was used to transmit Morse. He also took with him his camera as did many of his comrades.

It was not long before Steiniger was witnessing the truly destructive powers of modern warfare. 'As we passed the mangled wreckage of Russian tanks I glanced inside one or two. The dead Russians were seated, fallen forward, their uniforms torn, drenched in blood.' It seemed to Steiniger, and indeed the rest of the German Army, that nothing could withstand the Nazi onslaught. His regiment headed for the Lithuanian–Latvian border. It was apparent to Steiniger that their *Blitzkrieg* was invincible, 'We came to a place where evidently our Luftwaffe had surprised the remnants of the Russian T-26 tank division during its retreat and wiped it out.' He recounts with candour the terrible death of a Russian soldier, 'His head was missing, except the tongue and jawbone.'

Steiniger and his comrades, at the end of June, crossed over into Latvia and on into Estonia, where he witnessed the Red Army's total disregard for taking prisoners. While other Wehrmacht units pressed on toward the elusive prize of Leningrad, Steiniger's division was left to clear the Russians from Estonia. He notes with interest that many surrendering Soviet soldiers claimed to be Ukrainians in the hope of receiving 'preferential treatment'. He also recalls the warm welcome received by the people of the Baltic States glad to be rid of the Red Army.

By the end of the year he was beyond the Volkhov River and found himself enduring temperatures of –30 °C. There he had to sit out the bitter Russian winter with inadequate cold-weather clothing. In the spring of 1942 the river flooded, inundating many of his division's bunkers. He was then granted leave for the very first time since being conscripted. When he returned to his unit, his company commander arranged an unauthorised ceasefire with the Russian company facing them. This permitted the men to enjoy three days of gloriously unhindered sunbathing.

The following year Steiniger was involved in the fierce battles around Lake Ladoga near Leningrad. His regiment went into action by bus! It was during this fighting that the god of war smiled on Steiniger. For although he was hit in the spine by shrapnel, miraculously he was not paralysed. The military surgeon, erring on the side of caution, decided not to operate and let Steiniger keep his souvenir. He later returned to his unit to learn of the loss of the German Sixth Army at Stalingrad. By the summer of 1943 it was apparent that the Red Army was determined to liberate besieged Leningrad whatever the cost. This, though, did not happen until early 1944.

The Red Army launched an offensive that crushed Army Group North on 14 January 1944 and finally forced the Germans away from Leningrad. Soviet forces contained in the Oranienbaum bridgehead also struck south, catching the ill-prepared 9th and 10th Luftwaffe Field Divisions. Disastrously the latter when it transferred to the Army's control lost its flak battalion armed with 88 mm guns, which also operated in an anti-tank role. This left the division without effective firepower with which to ward off Soviet tanks. Both divisions, after enduring a barrage lasting over an hour and involving 104,000 shells, rapidly collapsed into chaos. It fell to the 61st Infantry Division, under the direction of XXVI Corps, to hold the line.

The much depleted 61st Division only narrowly escaped destruction and at the end of January 1944 managed to withdraw to the Narva River. Amongst its ranks was Steiniger and his friends. Attempts were made to refit and reinforce the division, but by this stage it had lost many of its experienced veterans. Bolstering the survivors with the remains of the 9th Luftwaffe Field Division and a fresh infantry regiment sent from Germany did little to boost morale (other survivors from the 9th and 10th Luftwaffe Divisions were sent to join the 2nd Flak Division). Worse was to come, for in June 1944 the Red Army smashed Army Group Centre, liberating Minsk and putting itself on the road to Warsaw and Berlin. To the south it liberated Odessa and a great swathe of Ukraine.

By October 1944 Steiniger and his comrades were at Libau and were shipped to Gotenhafen and then travelled by train to Königsberg in East Prussia. Just as the Red Army commenced its assault on the German enclave, Steiniger by good fortune was sent on leave and was subsequently unable to return to his regiment. The 61st Division surrendered at Königsberg on 10 April 1945 having suffered 28,500 casualties throughout the course of the war. When his leave ended Steiniger travelled to Dresden to find the city devastated by the Allies' bombers. He was then sent to help defend Stiegau in Silesia, but was driven out by Russian tanks. Taken prisoner at the end of the war, he spent four days at Auschwitz before being sent to Siberia as a slave labourer. He did not return to Germany until 1949.

That Erhard Steiniger was later able to write with such candour is quite remarkable as he, like every other young man caught up in the maelstrom of the Eastern Front, was undoubtedly deeply traumatised by what he saw and experienced. He talks of 'the terrible images which imprinted [themselves] indelibly in my memory'.

Steiniger's memoir is now available in English for the very first time and I have no hesitation in recommending his insightful book. It is a fine translation supported by numerous remarkable photographs that chart not only Erhard's wartime career, but also the fate of the 61st Infantry Division.

Anthony Tucker-Jones

Preface

I BEGAN WRITING THIS AUTOBIOGRAPHY for my children, covering the period of my life from 1920 to 1949. I have neither glorified nor apologised for anything. I have no great adventures to recount, nor even really unusual experiences, perhaps even less than thousands of fellow sufferers from that era.

It has been my intention to compose my wartime account unvarnished, and exactly as I saw it as a thoroughly unheroic personality in the years from my twentieth birthday onwards, including significant occurrences and personal opinions of the time. Naturally I emphasise that in the light of my later knowledge and maturity, these views changed in many respects.

I conceived this book originally as a kind of chronicle for my family. I was motivated by spontaneous encouragement from readers of the manuscript amongst my circle of relations and friends to place the material on a broader footing. I have therefore written the truth as I saw it, and where I am relying on reports I have made that clear.

Erhard Steiniger
Nuremberg,
April 1981

Introduction

MY HOME VILLAGE OF LANGUGEST (today Jenišův Újezd, map coordinates 50° 34' N 13° 43' E) lies in an extensive valley or perhaps better said a vast depression between the Erzgebirge mountains to the north-west and the Central Bohemian mountain range to the south and east. The population between the wars was 2,000.

When I was born there in 1920, the Czech state created by the victorious powers had been in existence for a year and a half. The Sudeten Germans had not been consulted. The slicing up of the German language area was carried out against the will of its inhabitants, apparently as part of the 'peace strategy' of the victors.[1] The reality was imposed by force of arms, and the dead of the March 1919 massacres put paid to any dreams of the Sudeten Germans that they were ever going to live in DeutschÖsterreich.[2] The Sudeten Germans were condemned in their totality to form over a fifth of the Czech population.[3] Now they had to come to terms with the new state of affairs. They were defenceless, bereft of their former rights, and faced a difficult political and economic future.

The Czech state decided that most German civil servants should be pensioned off so that Czechs could take over their positions. Only teachers at German schools and colleges remained in harness. All applicants for the civil service had to undertake to send their children to Czech schools and so prove their loyalty to the Czech state. German farms coming under the hammer in the period up to the economic crisis of 1936 were snapped up by Czechs, aided if need be by state funding. This policy of land transfers was aimed at further Czech-isation.

The former farmhouse at Langugest in the Bilin district of north-west Bohemia, the parental home where the author lived until called up in 1940. The photograph was taken in 1964.

Between Langugest, my home town, and Preschen (Břešťany) the government built the biggest and most modern brown-coal mine in all Czechoslovakia. Called the 'Masaryk mine' it employed Czechs from inner Bohemia. The German unemployed remained so, and lived on the weekly dole of ten *Kronen* which was enough

to buy 1. 5 kilos of sugar. In their spare time they roamed the coal dumps looked for anything combustible so as to keep warm in the winter.

I was the fourth child of five born to my mother. I took after her, and was the only one of her offspring with blue eyes. My father, invalided out of the Austrian Army in 1915 with a serious chest wound, owned 20 hectares of medium to good agricultural land, mostly down to cereals. We had two horses, eight cows, many geese and ducks and up to one hundred hens. It was one of the most progressive farming households of the locality and from 1928 we had a radio with loudspeaker and a gramophone. I began my primary education at age six, and attended a higher school at Dux from 1931.

31 January 1933 came. I learned of Hitler's 'seizure of power' on the railway platform at Preschen waiting for my train home. Simandl, a Czech schoolboy from the neighbouring village to whom I had never previously spoken, muttered under his breath, 'Hitler has become Reich Chancellor.' At my request he explained in halting Bohemian why this was so dangerous. A few days later we all knew about Hitler and the National Socialists: what good fortune they were going to bring to Germany, for example by cutting unemployment, and that Hitler was going to set aside the *Diktat* of the Versailles Treaty, and so on. German radio told us everything. Our esteem for the German Fatherland grew ever greater. Gone were any reservations my family might have had about the Nazis.

Bilin (Bílina) town and in the background the 538-metre clinkstone rock, the 'Borschen'.

The Erzgebirge in winter, scene at Neuhammer.

Typical Erzgebirge houses with shingle roofs.

Very nearly all of us Germans living on the Czech side of the Saxon border were thrilled by the news, either for feelings of nationality and race, or because in the German Reich there was bread and work, which the ruling Czechs had done their best to deny us. The aura of the new era was very strong and grew continuously, boosted by the radio broadcasts to which everybody tuned in. The Czechs outlawed the Nazi Party (NSDAP) and censored the mail of its operatives. Some time after this ban Konrad Henlein, a gymnastics teacher from Asch, founded a new party, the 'Sudetendeutsche Heimatfront', SHF for short. The Czech government took exception to the word 'Front' for its military connotations and forced the SHF to become the 'Sudetendeutsche Partei'. It became the catchment basin for all who had been forced into the Czech state against their will. What we wanted was autonomy based on the Swiss model since unification with Germany after the collapse of Austria-Hungary was forbidden by the Treaty of Saint-Germain.

Czechoslovakia at the time was peopled by six million Czechs, just over three million Germans, two million Slovaks, one million Hungarians and smaller numbers of other groups including Poles and Carpathian Ukrainians. There were no 'Czechoslovaks' as such, only Czechs and Slovaks, and the Slovaks were also striving for independence and freedom from Czech oppression. The best political solution might have been to create Czechoslovakia as a federal state on the Swiss model. The Czechs, however, a very nationalistic people, had been deluded by the victorious powers into believing that they could create a Czech state by vigorous Czech-isation. But the constituent parts were too large and could not be fitted together.

The inevitable result of Czech-isation was that the Sudetendeutsche Partei became the strongest in the Czech state. From 1936 onwards, it became increasingly clear that the party's push for 'autonomy' was merely a pretext for unification with Germany. An army of the unemployed from Bohemia crossed the border into Saxony seeking work – and found it. They became weekend commuters. Although in the main the work involved helping build autobahns, it was a livelihood much better paid in cash and kind than jobs available in Czechoslovakia. Germany had always been the world leader in social welfare legislation. The desire for unification with the Reich increased not only for nationalist-racial reasons but on these grounds too.

My sister Mimi (Marie, born 1911), my mother and I were the family members on the side of Henlein's Sudetendeutsche movement. Under pressure from my father as I neared school-leaving age, I applied to the Commercial College at Brüx. In those days there were no psychological tests or analysing people for their future development along the chosen career path, and so I went to Brüx, passed the entrance examination and from September 1934 my best friend Erich Müller and I made the round trip of twenty-six kilometres each day on our bicycles.

I would mention here that at Commercial College Professor Klaussner was Jewish, but there was no hatred of the Jews. Our family bought at Jewish shops and we were always satisfied customers. Professor Klaussner survived the period of the Third Reich and after the war lived in East Berlin.

On 28 June 1936 I received my diploma, which also served as my school-leaving certificate. My most important subsidiary subject, shorthand, was to stand me in good stead later. Now I faced the very difficult task of finding a job. A Sudeten German had next to no chance of being offered a position in public service, and industry was in dire straits. In his capacity as a member of the warehouse association's supervisory board at Bilin, my father had a quiet word with the Director, then I had a brief interview with the Director, and a few days later a letter arrived offering me a position as an unpaid probationer commencing on 1 August 1936. After working as a book-keeper for five months without remuneration, from January 1937 I was paid a pittance of 100 *Kronen* a week, equivalent to 12 *Reichsmarks*, but received a raise to 300 *Kronen* twelve months later, which was good money for an eighteen-year-old warehouseman in Czechoslovakia.

By 1938 the political situation in the Sudetenland was coming to a head. The Sudetendeutsche Partei had become the strongest single party in Czechoslovakia and had practically absorbed all the other German parties to the last dregs. My elder brother Oskar (born 1912) had joined the party secretly and I subscribed to it on my eighteenth birthday in April 1938. My father, a former standard-bearer for the Social Democrats, remained openly opposed until the day when Gustav Hacker, leader of the Farmers' Federation (Bund der Landwirte), returned from talks with Hitler and at a dramatic session in Prague convinced the managing committee of the federation to merge with the Henlein party. Soon after I saw my father taking its flag and treasury to the local

Probischtor in the sandstone mountains of the Elbe on the Bohemia–Saxony frontier.

Volcanic cones of the Bohemia central mountain range (at the right the Rosenberg).

Sudetendeutsche Partei chairman, but as far as I know he never joined.

The political tensions between Czechs and Germans grew in 1938 thanks to the intransigence of President Beneš. If he had ever entertained the idea of giving the Sudeten Germans autonomy, it

was by now too late and everybody except the Czechs knew that. Elsewhere Hitler had promised: 'The world should know that ten million Germans beyond its borders are no longer unprotected.' As usual, on this occasion the streets were deserted: the German community sat at home listening to the radio broadcast. By this figure of ten million, Hitler was referring directly to Austrians and for the first time to Sudeten Germans.

Afterwards at Bilin the population came spontaneously to the market square and sang the German national anthem until the Czech police arrived to break the crowd up. In May 1938, the Czech Army made its first partial mobilisation. The armed civilian land army patrolled the streets of the German neighbourhoods at night. The defensive installations, a staggered concrete-bunker system on the Czech–German border, ran along the heights south of our community and the troops there were put at immediate readiness. From there the Czech Army had everything in its field of fire as far as the Erzgebirge.

On my way to work one morning I was stopped and searched by armed civilians on a bridge near Bilin. I had no idea of what they hoped to find. The wearing of white socks, the outward sign of belonging to the German community, was discontinued after people identified by their socks were subjected to beatings while passing through mixed communities.

Meanwhile Austria had 'returned home to the Reich' to the great jubilation of the population (although nowadays under the pressure of political correctness this is unashamedly denied). We noticed as time went on that our cause provided the German Reich with its opportunity, and the relationship between Czechs and Sudeten Germans deteriorated accordingly. A Czech reign of terror began.

The Czech press was amongst the front runners: 'We are going to plaster the streets with German heads.' People were forced to skulk to work by a roundabout route to avoid confrontations; many decided not to go at all. Armed gangs roamed the streets at night knocking on doors. In August it was our turn. Armed civilians demanded of my parents at gunpoint that they deliver to them my younger brother Franz and his key to the community office. Franz belonged to no party, overflowed with kindness and goodwill to his fellow human beings and in the community office gave help and assistance to whoever needed it irrespective of origins or nationality. We discovered later that he had been transported with over 500 hostages from the Bilin district to the cellars of a brewery in the Czech town of Unhošt where all were informed that they would be drowned as a reprisal 'if the balloon goes up'.

Meanwhile, under the terms of the Czech mobilisation, my brother Oskar was called up for the dragoons at Komorn, Slovakia. During these weeks my mother wept bitter tears. She hoped and prayed that the Germans would invade. 'Why don't they just come? These people are not so strong as they make out.'

The Czech military had now occupied the lines of bunkers on the heights above our village and we no longer ventured into the fields. They were digging infantry trenches, putting up barbed-wire entanglements, bringing in anti-tank guns and rounding up all males able to wield a pick and shovel. Our village was on the main forward battle-line.

In order that I should dodge the draft, my mother packed me off to my elder married sister Mimi, who hid me in a small room. All radio sets had long been confiscated by municipal officials to deny us knowledge of events in the outside world. Mimi was well informed, however; she knew somebody in the neighbourhood who had a second radio and thus she kept me up to date with the political developments. In this way I learned of Hitler's dramatic speech in which he said, 'Here I stand and on the other side Herr Beneš. I call out to the world: "War or Peace?"' and so on. What a glimmer of hope it was for us at that time! The corresponding issue of the newspaper *Brüxer Zeitung* had a banner headline 'Hitler Speech' but the rest was left white – the Czech authorities had censored the whole thing. This told us enough. Therefore we had not been abandoned and left to our fate.

In the same way I learned of the Munich Conference[4] in which agreement had been reached as to the annexation of the Sudeten-German territories; for argument's sake the Czechs stalled about giving up the Dux and Brüx coal mines voluntarily. At that I thought it would be safe to return home by the back roads; on the way I was warned, 'Keep a good lookout, they are still picking up men for trench digging.'

On 9 October we needed brushwood to decorate the house. This meant going into the pine forest at Ganghof, passing between the military bunkers. We found most of the soldiers there to be Hungarians and Slovaks, as anxious for their liberation as we were, and they showed no interest in us.

Sunday 10 October 1938 was the day of our liberation. We went dressed in our Sunday best to the main road along which our liberators would be coming. From afar we could hear the church bells at Bruch and Oberleutensdorf ringing out their message of greeting. The houses were decorated and beflagged and as the column approached we could hardly believe our eyes – Czech military were leading them! A Czech tore down the flag from a house front and stuffed it in his field pack. The Czech company was followed by military motor-cyclists – and these looked quite different! Coal-scuttle steel helmets, field-grey uniforms, the eagle and swastika – Germans! Only a hostage who has lived under

foreign domination and feared for his life can know the feeling of happiness and joy we all experienced that day.

The Czech company commander refused to disarm his troops. Two German anti-tank guns passed us and secured the road to the east. At the same time, German machine gunners set up their weapons. Now the first Czech soldiers left the ranks with hands raised, shouting '*Magyar!*' Then the others followed suit, were disarmed and allowed to proceed to the demarcation line. We were free! Free to live in peace, speak our mother tongue, have public offices staffed by Germans. There was no longer a frontier with Germany. We could go to Bavaria, the Rhineland, Saxony and even East Prussia without a passport.

The Munich Agreement was not an injustice, a wrong, as is pretended today. Only areas with a predominantly German population were annexed and otherwise the Czech state lost no territory. That is the fact of the matter, every other allegation is nonsense invented to serve modern political purposes. This area was settled by Sudeten Germans in times immemorial, and was cultivated and industrialised by our ancestors. What the Czech economy lost was the industry within the German districts. Following the annexation there was no pogrom and the social democrats were not persecuted, although most thought it wise not to join the party.

The annexation of the Sudetenland was sealed by a plebiscite in October 1938. I do not doubt that 97 per cent voted in favour.

The Elbe Valley at Wannow near Aussing.

Our family now had German nationality. My brothers Oskar and Franz returned.

One evening in early 1939 I attended a meeting of members of the Sudetendeutsche Partei, the first and last time I ever did. Here I signed a form which made me automatically an applicant for membership in the NSDAP. This was approved and I received a Party number in the low 800,000s.

When war came in September 1939 there were sceptics, but the lightning victories in Poland and France, and the Non-Aggression Pact with the Soviet Union, calmed their fears. For the first year of the war I had a reserved occupation and was not conscripted into the Wehrmacht. As a book-keeper in the high season, especially around Christmas, I had had to help out estimating the quantities of cereals and grain delivered, and this gave me an insight into quality control. I learned about hectolitre weights, glassiness, gluten content and so on. This knowledge was very useful to me when, at the outbreak of war, the warehouse-keeper of our branch at Liebenshausen, who usually made the provisional returns, was conscripted into the Wehrmacht at short notice. I took his place until late 1940 when the Wehrmacht launched a major conscription drive during the course of which I was deprived of my reserved occupation status and drafted into the German Army.

Introduction Notes

1. Until the end of the First World War, an area of Bohemia and Moravia known as the Sudetenland had been part of Austria-Hungary. The peace treaty accepted by defeated Austria at Saint-Germain on 10 September 1919 recognised the new state of Czechoslovakia. The treaty forbade expressly the union of Austria with Germany and redrew the border between the two so that the entire Sudeten area fell into Czechoslovakia. Austrian officials unavailingly protested the violation of the principle of self-determination in the treaty and the arbitrary placement of three million ethnic Germans under Czechoslovak rule. *Trans.*
2. These were massacres committed by the Czech state on 4 March 1919 at Kadan (17 killed) and Sternberk (15 killed) to put down a general strike in the German-speaking provinces. *Trans.*
3. The February 1921 census showed that 3,123,000 persons had German as their first language; they formed 23.4 per cent of the population. *Trans.*
4. The famous Munich Agreement signed on 30 September 1938 was a settlement reached by Germany, Great Britain, France and Italy which permitted the German annexation of the Sudetenland. Czechoslovakia had no say in the negotiations. In March 1939 Hitler annexed the remainder of the country. *Trans.*

CHAPTER 1

From Conscription to the Memel Front

ON 12 OCTOBER 1940, with my call-up papers in my pocket and a packed suitcase, I boarded the train for Prague and my onward destination Beraun. I was the second member of our family to be conscripted into the Wehrmacht; my brother Franz had served with the artillery in the French campaign, and I thought then that the only possible next enemy must be Britain. Why else would they want soldiers? All other enemies lay defeated, and we had a non-aggression pact with the Soviet Union. My only anxiety therefore was that I might be being called up too late to see action.

I toured Prague for a couple of hours while awaiting my connection to Beraun: at my destination I headed as directed to the motor pool barracks where I was to join the signals: Infanterie Nachrichten Ersatz Kompanie 21 (21st Infantry Signals Reserve Company). I contented myself with the knowledge that I would not have much marching to do.

This was my first misconception, for there was a great difference between the 'signals troops' and 'troop signals', and I had been drafted to the latter. The signals troops were those units which maintained signals communications from the Wehrmacht higher staffs down to divisional level. For them as a rule the advanced front line was the regimental command post. On the other hand, the troop signals people were infantrymen wearing the 'lightning flash' badge on their sleeves, who maintained communications between regiment and battalion, and from there down to infantry companies. The signals troops were motorised, but the troop signals had to carry their radio equipment on their backs. There was an enormous difference between the two since the latter had much more exposure to enemy fire!

The second misconception was equally basic – the 'motor pool barracks' existed only as a phrase on the shield outside it. The sole motor vehicle inside was the provisions van. The deception was complete. I had not even passed fully through the barracks gate before I was made to hurry. A corporal liked to see new arrivals trot. 'Why are you creeping, man? Walk faster, what do you think you're here for? I'll build those legs up soon, rely on it!' This was not what I had expected my introduction to my personal role in the defence of the Fatherland to be like.

Once I was in the recruits' reception area everything took the prescribed course known to army recruits everywhere. At intervals other batches of recruits arrived. At the clothing store we were issued steel helmet, rifle, gas mask and identity disc. I was impressed at how forthright was the explanation provided here as to the purpose of the disc. The image of ending up on some battlefield torn to shreds did nothing to assuage my creeping doubts about serving the nation in this role.

Training began on the third day. After hearing tests, the recruits were divided into telephonists and telegraphists. I was sent to the room for the latter. The training for telegraphists was easier. While the telephonists had to dash across country carrying heavy rolls of cable on their backs, we sat comfortably in a warm room learning Morse code. This was fun and made us forget the 'welcome' inflicted on us during the previous two days.

So, what kind of people did I have to mix with? I got to know two or three boys from Saxony who enjoyed modern music as I did, and we imitated instruments with nose and throat when washing our fatigues in the evening in the laundry room. The others, taciturn, with harsh accents, were the East Prussians. When they talked among themselves it was incomprehensible to the listener. Strange people! They kept their own company, spoke little and watched everybody else mistrustfully out of the corner of an eye. Those here came from Elbing and Braunsberg. I vaguely remembered hearing about East Prussia during school geography lessons: I knew it was the granary of Germany, Tilsit had marvellous cheeses and the Trakehnen region had outstanding equine stud farms. Obviously I did not know then that my future troop would consist primarily of 'such people', nor that for the rest of my life I would never be able to relinquish them.

Our platoon leader was a small, wiry sergeant from Braunsberg, Unterfeldwebel Grossmann. On the final parade he called to me, 'You there in the third rank. You look very pale, you should have a shit.'

'*Jawohl, Herr Unterfeldwebel*, I should have a shit.' The old soldier from the Weimar 100,000-man army was right. The field-kitchen diet brought with it a five-day spell of constipation. Once I was cured I lost my pallor. My feeling of bodily well-being returned. After learning saluting we were allowed out of barracks and could go to the cinema.

Our stay in Beraun lasted six weeks. At the beginning of December 1940 we were kitted out with field dress and marched to the railway station. I hid my guitar under my greatcoat and got through the main gate in the centre rank without it being spotted. The train pulled out the same night and headed through Bavaria for France, stopping at Nancy, Le Mans and Rennes. It rained incessantly. In the Breton town of Quimper we were unloaded and waited to be fetched by somebody from our new unit. I was to remain with it until January 1945.

Signals Platoon, 151st Infantry Regiment

From Quimper station we were led to a portal beyond which lay a courtyard at the rear of the Hôtel Pascal. We paraded after a fashion to be welcomed by a *Feldwebel* (sergeant) as the senior NCO, accompanied by an *Unteroffizier* (corporal) and two rankers who were reserved but not unfriendly. The *Feldwebel* was a small and thin young man, pale and almost delicate looking, blond and blue-eyed, his hair cut strictly to military length. His field cap sat two fingers' width above his eyebrows as prescribed by regulations and had not the slightest degree of slant. His voice was clear and almost soft but rose when military harshness demanded it. He gave the new draft the once-over almost with a look of pleasure at seeing us. He stood before me and my guitar. 'I suppose you've come far?' I agreed that I had. 'Good!' Apparently he thought that I would be singing hiking and folk songs with the instrument, but he would have been disappointed to discover later that I knew only the latest hits. Our platoon leader was on the whole likable, and despite a certain comic aspect was respected by all of us.

We were allotted quarters in the guest house situated in the courtyard. Each room had six beds and a fireplace for which the hotel supplied firewood. It was without doubt a privilege to be billeted here as recruits. Our further training lay in the experienced hands of the sergeant and an *Obergefreiter* (lance-corporal) of the regimental signals platoon. They had always to be addressed using the formal version of the pronoun 'you'. They were 'veterans' who had fought in Poland and France; they were now our instructors and so our superiors. First of all the draft was separated into regimental signals platoon and battalion squads. I went with five others to the telegraphists of the signals platoon, without question another stroke of luck for me, the value of which would first be seen in the field. With these comrades I was to spend the next four years and so I shall provide a brief description of each here.

Werner Zahn, in the upper tier of the neighbouring bed, was tall, black-haired and squinted a little, particularly when thinking hard. He had an almost Mediterranean appearance but came from Rössel in East Prussia and spoke German without an accent except for a strong guttural 'r'. Werner was a calm, tolerant and altogether decent type and never got annoyed at practical jokes.

Gustav 'Pat' Wachnowski was slim, had a yellowish complexion and wore his long black hair combed back, which others thought ugly. He was an East Prussian from Neidenburg, no longer so young, peaceable and very decent. They were all decent, my comrades-in-arms, naturally with certain individual variations, after all we had different parents and origins.

Werner Zutraun had the *Abitur* – the school-leaving certificate, which qualified him for university: a dark type, could have been a Southerner, looked thoroughbred, came from Zoppot. He was very intelligent but liked to overawe all non-*Abitur* people with his intellectual superiority. All in all he was a brave soldier but had one shortcoming; he would not tolerate as God-given the chicanery of the lance-corporal hierarchy and later, in collusion with Pat Wachnowski who gave him support, he incited the other recruits to 'passive resistance'. This resulted in repeated punishment drills, for the hierarchy had, and ultimately had to have, the longer arm.

Werner Haferbier from Saxony was healthy and good-looking, outgoing like many Saxons and lively. Right from the start he was liked, though perhaps not always entirely upright and honest.

Later Heinz Schimanski joined our club, coming from the carrier pigeon post at Saint-Malo. Broad-shouldered and of average height with a rather odd nose, he originated from Königsberg and had the *Abitur*. During the first two years of the Russian campaign he would be my troop leader. He was a cynic, extremely knowledgeable, highly musical and a gifted linguist – he spoke perfect French. He was also an excellent sketch artist specialising in women, French style, preferably naked or scantily clad. He sang French songs and hits such as '*J'attendrai*' with all stanzas. Even deep in Russia he would declare passionately his love for France, but by that he probably meant his love for French women.

Our three instructors all had the rank of *Obergefreiter* and all came from East Prussia. Bruno Paukstadt, a theology student from Tilsit, had a wonderful baritone voice; Viktor Presch from the Ermland kept his private life to himself but had a sense of humour and was a brave, reliable soldier. The star of our telegraphy instructors was Ernst Skambraks, a hairdresser from Königsberg, a tall, lanky wearer of spectacles, jester and elocutionist, a specialist unbeatable in verses about landladies. He established a very good relationship with us young soldiers and for his trouble received an admonition from the higher powers for using the informal pronoun with us. The rules were very strict there!

A German regimental signals platoon of the Second World War had an officer as platoon leader. Below him would be a *Feldwebel*, five *Unteroffiziere* spread over four radio teams, two telephone construction teams and the switchboard operators. Additionally there would be some ZbV (special purposes) people, as I recall about thirty-three men in all.

Quimper in Brittany is a very fine small town and for German soldiers still under training in wartime we enjoyed a relatively good life, immeasurably better than at Beraun. At the beginning of December 1940 one *Reichsmark* was worth twenty French *francs*, which bought a lot here in 1940. One kilo of oranges cost eighteen *francs*, a bottle of Martell cognac sixty *francs*. At the weekends we ate in groups at the Hotel Pascal or the girls' boarding school. Typically the menu would be seafood *hors d'oeuvres*, two courses of fish or meat with boiled or fried potatoes, fruit for dessert and a glass of red wine. The bill would run to 95 *Pfennigs*, not even one *Reichsmark*!

Quimper had a mild climate by reason of its westerly position and the Gulf Stream so that date palms grew to a height of five or six metres. Layered stone walls protected the fields against storms from seaward; the surrounding hedges and trees were often entwined with ivy, mistletoe and other parasitic plants. Breton girls and women in traditional dress with snow-white upright cylindrical lacy headwear of various sizes depending on family status formed part of the landscape. Also beautiful were the stone churches and chapels.

The Odet Canal flowed through Quimper to the Atlantic. Our 61st Infantry Division was responsible for coastal protection in the area, the battalions of our regiment being stationed around Audierne and Douarnenez, fine fishing villages with sandy beaches enclosed on each side by the steep rocky coast. On 1 February 1941 we had the opportunity to visit the Pointe du Raz, one of the most westerly points of mainland France. Impressive small islands projected from the sea nearby like rocky mounts.

Occasionally waves as high as a house would come rolling in. I was tempted to clamber across the rocks to explore a fissure which had caught my eye. Fairly at its end once inside I noticed a kind of zoophyte, perhaps a sea anemone, which had taken hold in the rock floor. It was my first acquaintance with the sea and I cut off several of the plants with my pocket knife. Just as I was putting them in my haversack I heard Pat shouting my name urgently from above. Only then did I become aware of the giant wave approaching me and reacted instantly, clinging to the rocky floor with hands and feet and pressing my back against the ceiling of the grotto. When the wave reached me it lacked the force to sweep me out. I endured a following wave before scrambling apelike to safety, 'fear lending wings to my scurrying feet'. I dried off before the fireplace of a lonely stone cottage.

A few days after our arrival at Quimper we received a 'front supplement' of 420 francs to last ten days. Werner reappeared a short while afterwards asking if anybody could lend him ten *Reichsmarks*. His explanation of why he was broke led us telegraphists to an address at Rue du Jardin 4. It was the first time any of us had ever visited a brothel and I have to admit that for a relatively unspoiled Sudeten boy it was a revelation.

At the entrance the *madame* worked the beer pump and then we found a corner table in the gloom from where we could observe the proceedings. The air was thick with cigarette smoke, a general haze and perfume. There were groups of men present from Organisation Todt, various Army branches and the Kriegsmarine. We saw a naval man fondling a girl's breasts quite openly. Another girl was performing a provocative dance dressed only in net lace, and in some cases the ladies made their own selection – '*Du, Kamerad – komm!*'

Fritz Kesch at our table was captured in this way and so he was left behind when our group vacated this sexual first-aid post. It was mainly the married 'older' men used to their daily bread who made use of this establishment. We youths were still too respectable or cowardly to give it a try, although I make no claim to being a moralist.

In the Café de Paris we found pretty and friendly waitresses and a three-man orchestra, often assisted by our motor-cycle despatch rider Reinhold Kind with accordion. German, British and American hits were all popular here. It was an unwritten rule that this restaurant was reserved for officers from 2200 hrs. This did not worry us; we were happy to keep ourselves to ourselves with a cup of coffee or a beer. Reinhold, a talented jazz musician, was the only son of wealthy Rhineland parents. He often gave us much pleasure during the Russian campaign with his music. Although he had his *Abitur* and was qualified to be an officer he had no desire to be one and remained a despatch rider with our regimental staff. In 1943 when high casualties amongst the officers led to a promotion being forced upon him, he was reported missing during his probationary period with an infantry company and not heard from again.

In 1940 I had my first Christmas away from home. Towards 1600 on Christmas Day we were marched to the glorious Quimper cathedral for a religious field service held by army chaplains of various denominations. Before describing our Christmas celebrations I would like to mention our sergeant, Feldwebel Schumacher. Despite his weedy stature he was a soldier imbued with energy and will-power none would have expected of him. Even old soldiers who had known him as a *Gefreiter* respected him highly. If we came across him in town, our right hands would fly up smartly to our field caps and he would return the salute in the same way, and not casually as was the habit of all other higher ranks. (In the Wehrmacht, all persons of superior rank to oneself had to be saluted, not only officers.)

On another occasion, together with Obergefreiter Skambraks, he led us on a field exercise in which we had to assemble Dora 2 radios under battle conditions. It was not only Schumacher's adroitness in accomplishing this which impressed us but more so that he threw himself down in the mud with us when we came 'under fire'. He never asked us to do something which he was not prepared to do himself. He aimed to set us an example, and did so.

After dinner at Christmas 1940, Pat Wachnowski was to play 'Silent Night' on the violin alone and unaccompanied. He had had years of training on the instrument and the piece should have given him no problem. We all sat waiting around the Christmas tree, Pat put the violin to his chin – and his nerve went. It was the most dreadful rendering of the hymn imaginable. We could hardly keep a straight face, but not Feldwebel Schumacher. He sat throughout with a deadpan expression as if he were listening to Beethoven's Fifth, and even when he thanked the red-faced Pat for the musical rendition and then delivered his Christmas address.

Another memory of this Christmas celebration is having to carry the mulled claret from the field kitchen in cans and buckets. I was unable to understand a word of what our *Tross* (rearward services) people called out to us. They were East Prussian peasants who spoke their own dialect amongst themselves. At first when I heard it I thought they were Flemish or Dutch, certainly not Germans, but over the course of months and years I gradually came 'even to understand what we tell you'.

While we were lying abed making light conversation that night, Willi Gerk came into our dormitory. He had had too much to drink and tears ran down his cheeks as he unburdened his heart. 'Comrades, it is going to get terrible,' he said. He meant the invasion of England, now postponed until 1941. In the previous summer the regiment had taken part in practice embarkations on fishing boats. For Willi, this was not the booze talking but his

The Memelland district, lost to Germany under the Treaty of Versailles in 1919, was reincorporated into the German Reich by a treaty more or less forced on Lithuania on 22 March 1939, the last of the former German settled areas brought under Hitler's control without an armed invasion.

real concern for the future. What had Oberleutnant Rapreger said on his brief visit to our Christmas celebration? 'The year 1941 will present us with great tasks to perform. And that should make us pleased, for we shall have something to experience.' Rapreger was the regimental adjutant, in appearance and manner an officer figure straight from some propaganda film.

Willi Gerk had a premonition that he would not live long after that Christmas. At that time of course we still had no idea that the Soviet Union was next on the agenda for attack, and nor did we even know for sure until the day it happened. At the beginning of February 1941 when we were marched to the station and loaded aboard cattle trucks, we had no idea of our destination until we got there. Several days later came the order, *'Labium! oot-stiege!'* The voice of the Labiau stationmaster did not sound very French. We climbed down from the warmth of the cattle truck in which we had been crammed and into the freezing cold of East Prussia.

In East Prussia

We had arrived in the depth of winter. Snow half a metre deep covered the land and an icy wind swept the fields and roads. With heads drawn in we plodded towards Gross-Scharlack, a farmstead about six kilometres from Labiau. Quarters were allotted us in a little school. Oh how bitter was the change in our fortunes! With nostalgia we remembered the warm climate of Brittany with its large, almost warm drops of rain and the hotel room with its fireplace where we had lodged. Purchases and other pleasures were now a thing of the past.

The farmstead had about 2,000 acres of land with a dozen low-built little houses and stables. Here we had to make ourselves at home for a while. Hardly anybody was about, but unknown to us we were already being studied from behind curtains.

A few days later while we were cleaning our pots and pans at the village spring, a broad-shouldered man of short stature came to say, 'I've heard that you soldiers like baked potatoes.' Upon seeing our enthusiastic nods of agreement he pointed to his little house and introduced himself as the gardener Witt, inviting us to enter. It was amazing that we could all find space in that cottage to sit. A huge deep bowl full of crispy baked potatoes stood waiting for us. I don't think that the French meals served at the girls' boarding school in Quimper tasted better! The small, roundish Frau Witt, former cook at the farm, often gave us the opportunity later to admire her cooking. The following Sunday we telegraphists were invited for éclairs. The entire regimental signals platoon could not constantly take advantage of the hospitality of these people and so each man contributed a 20 *Reichsmark* note, cash being in short supply with the Witts as it was with all farmworkers.

This was our first contact with the 'reserved' East Prussian people on the land. Gardner Witt also arranged entertainment for us in our spare time. He cleared out his hothouse, a corrugated-iron structure 5 × 12 metres, to make a dance hall. Werner provided the music with his small accordion and I with my guitar; a local boy aged about fifteen joined in with a harmonica. We named the place 'Café Wellblech' which means 'corrugated iron' and it gave both the locals and ourselves a lot of fun. The contact with these simple people was unforced and well-behaved on both sides.

The warning given by Leutnant Schumacher, who had meanwhile been made up from *Feldwebel*, not to turn the girls' heads with our sophistication, was unnecessary, for by nature and upbringing we preserved the proprieties.

The Gross-Scharlack idyll came to an end at the beginning of April 1941. Things had begun to look serious, and so I made a gift of my guitar to the Witt's daughter ('the young girl with a child's face'). Rumour had it that the Russians were going to open a corridor for us down to Persia so that we could eject the British from there.

On the evening before we pulled out the estate owner treated us to a lavish farewell with baked potatoes and sausage. Gardener Witt was indignant and referred to him as a 'cheapskate' and

The Königin-Luise Bridge at Tilsit with the Memelland spreading away in the background.

Above: Nidden on the Kurische Nehrung (or Curonian Spit), a peninsula of land and dunes 98 kilometres in length separating the Kurisches Haff (Curonian lagoon) from the Baltic. The photograph was taken from the Schwiegermutterberg elevation, known pre-war for the house built on it by the writer Thomas Mann.

Top right: Traditional wooden flat-bottomed sailing canoes on the Kurisches Haff. These canoes fished in pairs dragging a net.

Right: The market place at Suwałki in occupied Poland was used regularly for the sale of produce from outlying farms.

something else, motivating his daughter to exclaim 'Papa!' and so what he added must have been much stronger. Next evening we marched out accompanied by young and old part of the way. They left us with their good wishes, more thought than spoken.

We marched by night to the north-east. I quite enjoyed it. I had no problem walking for hours particularly with the stimulating silhouette of the moonlit fir-woods frequently alongside us. Silence, glorious silence! The soldiers' songs we sang at the outset gradually died away and our steady plod reverted to marching in step. Marching in the monotony of step and body movement is easier and more sparing of energy. One can simply switch off the mind and even the noises of the marching body are no longer perceived knowingly. Only now and again a sudden snort from one of the heavy grey horses pulling the radio waggon at our rear brought back the present and gave us at the same time the sense of their indissoluble loyal friendship. These brave horses deserve their own chapter. They suffered and died as did the men to whom they had become true comrades.

We stopped at Schillen for a few days. Here again we practised our telegraphy communications in the field under simulated battle conditions. I was assigned to the troop led by Unteroffizier

The approaches to the Königin-Luise Bridge at Tilsit, probably 1941.

Bruno Paukstadt. Wherever he took us he was guaranteed to find some shop or pharmacy with a liquor licence. He liked us to have a schnapps inside us. We found him to be a thoroughly equable and well-balanced man and humanitarian who found the chicanery practised by many recruit-instructors deeply repugnant. 'Live and let live' was his motto.

Tilsit on the Memel in East Prussia, a photograph taken from the Königin-Luise Bridge.

On 8 April 1941 I celebrated my twenty-first birthday at Schillen. This celebration consisted of a pear liqueur in a hotel on the market place, this being a day off for me. I also wrote a nice letter to my parents thanking them for everything they had done for me for now I had come of age and could make decisions independently, or so I thought. As it was, now and in the years

which lay ahead, I was always subjugated unconditionally to this or that will. What other point did military training have but to teach unconditional obedience irrespective of all subjective emotions and considerations.

The longer-serving instructors up to corporal, who in civilian life had a manual trade or were unskilled, now enjoyed harassing across country the *Abitur*-holders or those similarly qualified. I mention Unteroffizier Salecker from Tilsit who became one of our instructors and in later years played a role which set the tone in the regimental signals platoon. Formerly we had not seen much of him. He was nicknamed '*Der Dicke*' – 'Fatty'; if he annoyed, bullied or persecuted us unjustly then he became 'the fat pig'. I never referred to him as such because I didn't have to put up with too much nonsense from him. He had a sense of humour but liked to pick on people. When he did it to me I would find an ironic response which he would accept with an embarrassed grin.

On 20 April 1941 our division crossed the Memel river by the Königin Luise bridge at Tilsit. Unknowingly I passed almost by the front door of the house where my future wife lived. On this march I obtained for the first time a visual impression of how many thousand men made up a division. Its infantry strength was easy to calculate but not everything that came along with it. By reason of the thaw the Memel had flooded its banks. We marched into German territory which had been liberated – the Memel-land.[1] This was the longest continuous

A typical terrace of houses in Memel (today Klaipėda in Lithuania).

march in which I ever took part as a soldier, more than 60 km. The following morning when we reached our quarters at the Burgomaster's we were tottering with fatigue but I had no blisters.

At the Matzigen estate our platoon was allotted the small school for our quarters. Heydekrug was nearby: I remember it not only for Sudermann's exciting tales, which I loved reading, but for a bad experience. In France I had once had too much Martell cognac so that now I could not even stand the smell of it. Here at Heydekrug I developed a great liking for schnapps. Heinz duped me and on the way home I was sick as a pig and worse. One good thing came from it, however; never again in my life did I get stupidly drunk, for now I knew my limit.

I do have one happy memory of Heydekrug. Before the Russian campaign, the regiment arranged for a steamer to leave there for the Curonian Spit, enabling us to see a piece of the beauty of this austere, original coast of Memelland. Our steamer crossed the lagoon to Nidden with its gigantic dunes and 'valley of silence', and, on the other side of the long spit of land, the Baltic Sea. It was not difficult to imagine what a glorious holiday spot this used to be with sand, sun, water, blue sky, mountain pines and much tranquillity.

Orders came for the division to move forward. We pushed slowly towards the north and the border, moving only by night. East of Memel the roads of the frontier country were camouflaged to the future enemy's view wherever necessary.

Leutnant Schumacher left us to be a 3rd Battalion staff officer under Hauptmann Rooch. Schumacher did not have it easy but passed the course. His replacement as our platoon leader was the former commander of the regimental signals platoon, Leutnant Dr Walther Hubatsch. The veterans of the platoon spoke his name with respect. We still had a few weeks before the Russian campaign in which we got to know him. He was an officer of average height, slim and with a military bearing. He smiled only rarely. A convinced, strict superior officer.

Sandy field paths in the Memel region.

I did not succeed in obtaining his approbation immediately. At a training class on the equipping of a troop unit he asked the class what was the best vehicle for our kind of work. I was the only person to raise my hand. My naïve response was '*Panjewagen*' – a horse-drawn cart. The face of my platoon leader which had beamed at me in happy expectation darkened suddenly. Before the laughter of my classmates had subsided, he thundered, '*Ja ja*, we shall all get on one and drive off.' The idea did not seem to me completely unreasonable. Naturally the German Army did not have official *panje* carts, only standard service vehicles – unfortunately! As our heavy steel-plated vehicles were to prove on the poor Russian paths and roads, particularly during the season of mud, they were completely unsuitable and in the course of the Russian campaign we were forced to adopt *panje* carts, at least partially.

Those days immediately before Barbarossa are worth some reflection. All doubts about our intentions had now been set aside. At regimental staff, maps of Lithuania, Latvia and Estonia lay open – our operational area. Feldwebel Kiausch showed us an Army information bulletin illustrating obsolete and primitive Soviet weaponry that had been captured by the Finns. 'Now there's a surprise,' he added. But very soon we were indeed surprised for the Russians had excellent modern weapons, in many cases superior to ours, such as the T-34 tank, not to mention the many types of modern and effective firearms. Our soldiers had to be equal to, and if possible superior to, the numerical and to some extent technical superiority of the enemy. This was to be achieved by courage, fighting spirit and self-sacrifice, therefore always at the risk of our lives.

On the bridge of a small frontier river a no longer quite so young soldier of our pioneer platoon stood resting his arms on the railings looking down into the water. I went to his side and stood with him, watching the tree trunks coming downstream from the other side. 'The Russians are still delivering then,' I said.

'Ho ho, many will lose sleep, comrade, if these trunks stop coming.' This prophecy gave me an ill-feeling.

Next evening, 21 June 1941, Hauptmann Dr Pankow, a dentist from Cranz, had the Headquarters Company parade, with sentries posted, to hear the latest Führer-Order: 'Under this heavy burden, I turn to you my soldiers asking you to take upon yourselves the active defence of the Reich.' He spoke of us being on 'the most gigantic front of all times' and so on. Hauptmann Pankow recommended that everybody who wanted to write home should do so now since there would be no time for it in the days ahead.

We of the regimental signals platoon were divided up for the imminent operation. I went as number 2 to Theo Rösler. There was no time for sleep: at midnight he and I went to the 3rd

Battalion readiness area. A farmer's wife was preparing fried eggs for officers of the battalion staff. How could they eat at a time like this? My stomach felt like a lump of lead. The civilian population was leaving the operational area and their homes with belongings on their backs.

Chapter 1 Notes

1. The Memel-land enclave beside the river of the same name had been Prussian territory until the end of the First World War but was detached by the Treaty of Versailles in 1919. It became part of Lithuania in January 1923. Eventually, after typical Hitlerian pressure on Lithuania, a treaty was signed on 22 March 1939 whereby Lithuania 'voluntarily' transferred Memel to Germany. Even before the treaty was signed Hitler arrived aboard the pocket battleship *Deutschland*, toured the city to great acclaim and made a short speech. *Trans.*

CHAPTER 2

Barbarossa – Lithuania

The Molotov–Ribbentrop Pact signed in Moscow on 23 August 1939, as amended by the Boundary and Friendship Treaty of 28 September 1939, contained secret protocols which amongst other territories allocated Lithuania, Latvia and Estonia to the Soviet sphere of interest. On 15 June 1940 the Soviets invaded Lithuania, and next day Latvia and Estonia. The three Baltic States were still under Soviet occupation when Operation Barbarossa began.

ON 22 JUNE 1941 AT 0315 HOURS our artillery opened fire. The grey dawn thundered with shellfire. Fear overcame me, I sweated, my stomach revolted. I tried not to show my anxiety. No doubt others were feeling the same; not everybody is born to be a hero. There was no more time left to reflect for scarcely ten minutes later we had to take up our equipment and follow the battalion staff.

To add to my misery I was also weighed down by the 17-kg radio apparatus case, plus gas mask, steel helmet, entrenching tool and the crazy carbine, which always interfered with progress. My Agfa-Isolette folding camera swung this way and that at every step. In this get-up Rösler and I headed across the Lithuanian fields through swathes of morning mist. No roads, no firm paths. The first bullets chirped around my ears. Involuntarily I drew in my head, pointless to do so, too late for that.

I noticed the originality of the battalion leader. He was not advancing half a kilometre behind the spearhead, but with the front line, at its centre. The leadership techniques of other commanders did not interest him. He wanted to see what was happening at the front. He had arranged our advance as follows: a mine-clearance

A unit of 61st Infantry Division receiving its orders, spring 1941.

A ride through Memel. At the centre Major Gottfried Weber, commander of 1st Battalion, 162nd Infantry Regiment.

party ahead, then a platoon of infantry with a skirmish line of riflemen and at the centre of these the battalion staff, to which Rösler and I were attached. In a fight with this heavy radio casing on our backs we would be useless.

On this very first day I saw that our Dora-2 equipment was not of an ideal design.[1] It was good for grinding down physically and mentally the telegraphists who had to struggle along with it. The equipment had a maximum range of fourteen kilometres, and this only on the flat, at sea or on a plain, and only when using the Morse key. As a 'walkie-talkie' one had to settle for three kilometres. The call came: 'Regimental telegraphist to me! Send: "Have crossed line XY, weak enemy resistance, advancing farther in direction Z." Make sure you have the connection quickly. We are going forward in that direction, if necessary I shall leave a messenger back at the end of the plain who will then lead you.'

We encoded the message and got our connection at once, the regimental HQ had not yet changed position. Scarcely had we received confirmation than we strapped on the cases again so as not to lose contact ahead, wary, for snipers were shooting from the woods. Now we looked for our battalion; we had only to follow the sound of fighting to catch up.

We dragged ourselves across the terrain for hours. The morning mist was long gone and now we passed burning thatched-roof cottages and other humble homesteads that had caught light like tinder when hit by the first bursts of tracer. Their black smoke marked the path of our advance. Struggling in a fairly exhausted condition to keep up with the battalion staff with all the gear I had to lug along, I was already sick to death of it on the first day. Then I heard a voice I knew well saying from above me, 'Ah! Propaganda Company man Steiniger. First class!' Leutnant Schumacher looked down at me with a smile and wished me 'Good photography!' Until then I had taken no photos, I was simply too exhausted. Was this sarcasm, calling me a Propaganda Company man on account of my condition of funk being visible to everybody?

An unidentified *Leutnant* of 162nd Infantry Regiment delivering an address.

Finally, in the afternoon we reached a well-laid highway along which the first Russian prisoners were arriving. One or two Russian 12.2-cm guns were firing sporadically on our supply route; splinters whirred around. I remember my father saying one day that all it needed was a single shell to explode close by to put an end to you. 'Father, you were right,' I thought.

I had now put my baptism of fire behind me on my first day of the Russian campaign. Even later into the war I never lost my respect for artillery. It needed only one gun somewhere, sometime, to fire in your direction and the shell would arrive unexpectedly. Aircraft bombs only fell while there were aircraft in the air to drop them, and one could then shelter, but artillery did not necessarily give a warning and next instant the shell would come hurtling over to explode where you stood or, if you were lucky, fell a hundred metres short or long to spray somebody else. The major splinter effect was felt in the direction of fire.

One needs luck in warfare, a lot of luck. Therefore I could never be a hero, of that I was certain. The Iron Cross would never adorn my chest, and more importantly I hoped no wooden cross with steel helmet perched on top of it would mark my grave. When we

The *Spiess* (Company Sergeant-Major) recently decorated with the Iron Cross, II Class.

The birthday of the officer at the centre of the group being celebrated with a glass of red wine, 1941.

halted again I fell asleep from exhaustion at the roadside. In the evening we were relieved and rejoined the regimental staff.

Next day, 23 June 1941, being needful of rest and recuperation, we were allocated two seats on a truck accompanying our signals vehicle. The regiment advanced without interruption even though the resistance of the Russians was increasing at each interception point. Werner Zahn was apparently enjoying the situation. 'The Russian is an outstanding tactician in retreat; he was a master of it in the First World War,' he reminded us whenever we had to pass within sight of another cleverly set blocking position, which our brave infantry were going to have to wipe out. In the next couple of days we took hardly any prisoners and only now and again did our transports come across a broken-down truck or tracked vehicle to remove for examination. Motorisation was the secret of the Russians' delaying tactics. They would disengage swiftly from battle and win time using a motorised retreat to build another strongpoint farther back. This gave them the additional benefit of having relatively well-rested soldiers for their defence.

On the second day of our campaign our rearward services – *Tross* – often came to a standstill. The Russian artillery was scattering fire along the road of advance. I was sitting near Feldwebel Kiausch at the roadside. A distant dull discharge – and in the same instant the *Feldwebel* pushed me into the roadside ditch just in time to escape the whirring splinters of the shell which exploded no more than four metres from us. The 'veterans' had previous experience by which they often judged by the sound of an artillery piece firing if the shell would come down dangerously near or farther away. 'Yes, youngster, you have to keep your head low when one goes off,' the *Feldwebel* said. He had saved my life or at least prevented me from being wounded.

The Russian resistance grew more determined. The wait for the *Tross*, which moved up behind the advancing infantry, was longer delayed. 'This is worse than in France,' I heard one of the veterans say. The unusually long bursts of heavy-machine-gun fire taught us that the situation for advancing infantry companies is not always easy. In these opening days we lost the first of our staff officers to fall in action, Leutnant Kragen, commander of the pioneer platoon. He was one of the men from the Weimar 100,000-man army, a pleasant man often seen riding a black horse.

At this point I would make the general observation that so far as I judged from experience the officers of our regiment whom I got to know were irreproachable, exemplary soldiers. In all my wartime service I can only remember one officer who dug his own slit trench as fast as he could and of whom it was known that he preferred to live rather than die a heroic death for the Fatherland. I liked him, but for obvious reasons the Army could not use such officers. Apart from this man I never knew a German officer who showed fear outwardly or was cowardly for even a second. I have the greatest esteem for the officers of the infantry corps of those

Memel harbour with two Kriegsmarine minesweepers at the quayside.

Resting by the wayside during an exercise, spring 1941.

days; they were simultaneously the superior officers and also comrades of the men placed under them and set an example in every situation. They were responsible for their sector and were not prepared to shelter in their trench when an artillery barrage was hammering our positions; they had to keep watch on the

sector so as to take counter-measures should the necessity arise. Accordingly the losses of officers in the infantry corps were unusually high.

On the evening of 24 June we were preparing to spend the night south of Piezai in an area of broken woodland and meadow when we heard the sound of heavy motors not too far away – beyond any doubt tanks. The order was passed orally to dig holes for protection. The rumbling was a warning that we were caught out in the open should any of those tanks stray our way. The Soviets had thrown a tank division into the battle. We had not a single panzer but a substantial number of 3.7-cm anti-tank guns.

The following two days showed us what keeping calm, iron discipline and a determined will to fight can achieve. Lilac smoke, now seen by day more frequently, warned of enemy tank activity and the call 'anti-tank gunners to the front' went down the line. The *Tross* vehicles vacated the left side of the road to enable the guns and men to move up. What 14th Company and elements of 161st Anti-tank Battalion would achieve over the next three days was heroic.

The Russian tanks were hunted down in the truest sense of the word. Our 3.7-cm guns advanced to the slightly higher ground on either side of the road, which the Russians would use for their retreat, took up their battle positions and opened fire at once when in range. Fortunately the tanks which our guns had to engage were 'only T-26s'.[2]

The anti-tank close combat weapons used later were unknown to us then if one discounts hollow-charge mines. Even so, on the first day of battle more than twenty of these tanks were destroyed. This was only the prelude. I was not aware of the overall position of the division, but I inferred from the nervousness at regimental staff that the regiment had been forced to set up an all-round defence and that a 'difficult situation' had begun to develop into a 'crisis'. The pioneer and mounted platoons had already been remustered as reserve infantry. Hauptmann Pankow said, 'Come up, boys, and bring ammunition forward.' The way he said this told me that we were in trouble. Finally our divisional artillery gave us the chance to draw breath so that the attack could be continued towards Piezai. As evening drew in we moved forward.

The onset of darkness and the hard, dry reports of anti-tank gunfire mixed with the flitting tracer of the Russian tank cannons lent excitement to the whole scene. However, it was not a war film but deadly serious and men had to die. The battle lasted all night. We two telegraphists spent the time in a warehouse near stacked cases of Lithuanian vodka. Next morning, 27 June, the regiment continued its advance. As we passed the mangled wreckage of Russian tanks I glanced inside one or two. The dead Russians were seated, fallen forward, their uniforms torn, drenched in

A company of 162nd Infantry Regiment formed up on parade.

blood; streams of blood had congealed on their faces, and hands and arms dangled by their sides. Their eyes were either closed or staring into endless infinity, their complexions waxy. I became still and pensive. How many of our own men looked like this or worse? The German dead we did not see, for where possible they would be quickly transported away.

I was specially impressed by an incident just at the exit to the village on the left side of the road. A Russian tank had gone

Men of 162nd Infantry Regiment at Suwałki posing before a synagogue with broken window panes.

A stroll in Suwałki, Poland, near the frontier with Lithuania.

for one of our anti-tank guns and crushed the gunshield before being destroyed a second later, apparently by a shell fired upwards into its interior through the floor plating. Whether our gunners survived this encounter was not known.

In those three days, the Russians lost more than thirty of their tanks around Piezai. Of these, Gefreiter Heinze of our 14th Company destroyed ten in twenty minutes. It appeared that the regimental staff had ventured too far ahead and been surprised by the Russian tank squadron. This had resulted in the need for our no longer young Oberst Melzer and his adjutant to crawl through a wheat field to get clear of the danger zone. It was a very hot day and the colonel was just wiping the sweat from his brow when a Soviet prisoner was brought up for questioning. This prisoner answered him as '*Tovarisch Kommandant*', after which the colonel enquired of his adjutant, 'Is that an honourable term or an insult?'

Next day our advance towards the Lithuanian–Latvian border continued in the direction of Mitau, in the Riga district. On the way we came to a place where evidently our Luftwaffe had surprised the remnants of the Russian T-26 tank division during its retreat and wiped it out. In the morning we had heard in the distance the unmistakable sound of aircraft bombs detonating and now we saw the results. Left and right of the highway used for their retreat and in the adjoining meadowlands lay the remains of the tanks which had attempted to flee using a star-shaped formation. To no avail, the bombs got them anyway. Between the tanks lay their wrecked supply vehicles and many dead Russians. At the crossroads, on a mound of earth, a dead Russian lay on his back, legs spread but at odd angles. His head was missing, except the tongue and jawbone. Ligaments and muscle flesh were stuck together by the dried blood. A bomb splinter had probably catapulted the head into the nearby field of rye. This man had died a hero's death, and this was what it looked like. On 28 or 29 June 1941 a stone marker informed us that we had reached the Latvian frontier.

Chapter 2 Notes

1. 'Dora-2' was the Torn. Fu. d-2 portable high-frequency VHF transceiver, a common infantry set. When it was being used on the move, one man carried the transmitter/receiver and the other the battery/power supply and handset. A cable linked the two men. Each pack was 31 cm high, 36 cm wide and 17 cm deep. The set pack weighed 16 kg, the battery pack 17 kg. *Trans.*
2. In 1941, the near obsolete Soviet T-26 light infantry tank formed the backbone numerically of the Red Army tank arm. Battle-ready weight: 10.5 tonnes, main armament 45-mm cannon, crew 3. *Trans.*

CHAPTER 3

Barbarossa – Latvia and Estonia

ON 28 OR 29 JUNE 1941 we crossed the frontier into Latvia. One could almost describe the region as cared for, or in any case clean and cultivated. The previous dirty grey mud huts of the Lithuanian peasants were exchanged here for wooden houses. The wheat was free of weeds and the quality on the haulm excellent. We might have been forgiven for feeling that this was like home and so our morale was good. The inhabitants greeted us as liberators.[1]

We followed the vanguard of I Army Corps in the direction of Riga. At Mitau we passed a captured Soviet military airfield. Here they stood, the silvery, nimble but too slow bumble-bees, the *Ratas* – Soviet fighters. They had fought to the last gasp. Our divisional staff had pressed on for Riga, 'Paris of the East', and set up quarters on the nearer bank of the Düna. Although the bridge over the river had been blown up, the vanguard had gained a foothold on the other side and established a bridgehead there. Our joy was short-lived, however. About ten kilometres from the Latvian capital the *Tross* columns had had to wait, fighting could be heard on both sides of the road and, particularly in the swampy woodlands, enemy infantry and artillery fire.

On the right-hand side of the road the German artillery were firing with all barrels. Scattered Russians amounting to about a regiment in strength were blocking our way into Riga and had to be wiped out at considerable cost to ourselves. The divisional staff had been cut off by these Russians, and then we surrounded them.

That evening, 1 July 1941, we marched into Riga. Earlier there had been rain but now it was sunny. We crossed the Düna to the northern part of the city in assault boats. The ruins of the

Russian barbed-wire obstacles on the Lithuanian frontier with Memel.

magnificent houses of several storeys, now gutted by fire, along the banks of the river received us with empty eyes. On that part of the demolished bridge that was still standing were three or four German armoured scout cars and light panzers. They had almost crossed the bridge when it was blown up. Right at the bridgehead was a battery of heavy Russian anti-aircraft guns, their long barrels pointing to the skies. A rag doll had been

stuffed into a muzzle brake, presumably by the Latvian militia. We saw a lot of them now, formed from elements of the former Latvian Army and civilians, now restoring order in their own way in liberated Riga. We radio operators were given lodgings in the large flat of a Latvian Jew. He seemed to be ill, and spent his time in his living room in a large leather armchair. Occasionally he tried to engage us in political conversation but we saw no point in it, preferring to spend the two days of our stay in Riga getting to know the city.

Riga looked like it had once been a German city. I could imagine the enthusiasm with which my platoon commander would inspect all the historical German structures at close quarters such as the Church of St Peter, begun in 1209 and the old Guild House of the Black Heads dating from the fourteenth century. We telegraphists of the regimental signals platoon entered a hotel *en masse* to be fed caviar on bread. It was the first and last time I tasted it in my life; the price for this moderate pleasure was too high. When returning to our lodgings I saw on the street victims being led off chained to shackles around their throats. Who these people were I never found out but no German soldiers were involved. All the same, now I understood the concerns of our host, who must have feared the same fate for himself.

Next day, 4 July 1941, we marched out to the north-east and met no resistance. Passing through Segewold and Wolmar we crossed the Estonian border into Walk and Fellin. Even enemy

aircraft left us in peace. On account of the searing heat we often stopped at farmhouses on the way to quench our thirst. The wells with their cool precious water were often poisoned. Therefore we preferred milk which the farmers' wives offered from large cans hanging in the wells. This cooled milk was refreshing and a real treat but it had its consequences for some: the doctors called it 'enteritis' but it was harmless.

Those days on the march, despite temperatures of up to 40 °C, and the great distance to be covered, were almost pleasant because we ran into no opposition and could sleep by night. The population was well disposed to us and welcomed us as liberators, particularly those who had had family members deported by the Russians. One day we found a Russian guitar with seven strings. One was removed and then we used the instrument to accompany our marches. One afternoon when we were signing '*Heidemarie*', the regimental commander's Volkswagen amphibious car slowed as it passed our column.

'*Heil*, signals platoon!'

'*Heil, Herr Oberst!*' we shouted back. Oberst Melzer smiled contentedly, apparently pleased at the high morale amongst his signals troops.

The telephone troop, which handled the setting up and removal of cabling, had not come up with us. The telegraphy team consisted of only two men each on call 24 hours, the second man being necessary for encrypting and decoding, and also sat on watch at

A unit of 61st Infantry Division advancing in June 1941.

the radio should our commander need to send or receive signals from the commanding officer or his adjutants. The signals platoon commander often passed the wiring jobs to battalion to allow overtired telegraphists to get a few hours' sleep. The battalion commanders were glad to have a field telephone available.

We regimental telegraphists were always welcome at 1st and 2nd Battalions, and the signals staff NCOs Oberfeldwebeln Schilwa and Reuter respectively, were always pleasant and attentive so that we always felt at home there. The commander of 3rd Battalion was very dependent on the field telephone because he liked to discuss the situation. Apparently he did not find it easy to reduce a situation to its bare essentials in brief phrases as was necessary in telegraphy. We did not like going to 3rd Battalion, there was always an unpleasant feeling about it that we were somehow nearer to death there. This didn't happen at other battalions. It was due not only to the way in which 3rd Battalion was led and the increased risks it held for us, but the impersonal attitude of the battalion commander towards us also contributed to this impression. He was more kindly disposed to the telephone squad.

As signals staff we often had contact with the battalion commanders and often came into possession of information not meant for general consumption. During our advance I was frequently at 1st Battalion and in the Volkhov position at 2nd Battalion, of which later. We all thought very highly of Major Budnick of 1st Battalion. We saw that he did not send people lightly into dangerous situations, that when giving his company commanders their orders he would always add a warning such as, 'Zonewitz' or 'Saint-Paul, take care, we don't know what is in that woodland.' These two company commanders had apparently taken the *Major* to their hearts. This feeling that their lives wouldn't be wasted uselessly was shared by the men. NCOs and men had a fine nose for that kind of thing.

Near Reval, the capital of Estonia, we were once witnesses – or rather listeners – to another not quite sober conversation. The battalion command post was the lighthouse. It was the target of Russian naval gunnery but no matter how often they fired they

Houses afire during fighting on the Lithuanian frontier, June 1941.

A column of smoke indicating the way to the front.

could never hit it. A start to the disembarkation of our fighting units had begun, we were almost certain of success and for this reason even some of the battalion staff had begun celebrating with the bottle. It was evening. In the company with the CO was that officer who was not able to conceal his fear when in action. I mentioned him earlier. We now heard how Major Budnick, contrary to his usual custom, spoke up so loudly that we regimental telegraphists in the neighbouring room could have heard everything if we had wanted to. We heard him shout, 'Sir! You do not belong in my Battalion. You are a lady-killer and philanderer!' I do not know how this conversation continued. Heinz Schimanski would certainly have known more. I mention this in order to emphasise the integrity of the man even in this area.

We had to advance. The days free of contact with the enemy came to an end. We reached the town of Fellin, which a little earlier had had to withstand a Luftwaffe air attack before our troops took it. The liqueur factory had escaped damage and remained in business. The exchange rate was one *Reichsmark* to ten *roubles* The purchases here were the first and last of their kind, for from now on the war became increasingly hard-fought.

Even at the divisional level we did not learn much about the overall situation except that the vanguard of our army corps had been disbanded. We did not have enough infantry to engage the Russian motorised units ahead.

The Estonians with their blue-black-white flags welcomed us as liberators as the Latvians had done previously. Estonian volunteers were assembled into auxiliary corps under the superintendence of a German officer but led by an Estonian commander. They were given special tasks which required native speakers, such as the neutralisation of Russian stragglers operating from ambush positions.

The topography of Estonia is hilly and more rugged than Latvia and for that reason more handsome. To the north we found it increasingly interspersed with giant boulders deposited there in the Ice Ages and therefore debris from Scandinavia. Personally I preferred Estonia to Latvia. The Estonian coast from the Gulf of Finland to the Bay of Riga, which I got to know better later in the war, reinforced the positive impression I had of this country.

Around 11 or 12 July we reached Pilistvere. Hauptmann Michalik and his horsemen (of the regimental mounted platoon) were sent to cleanse some fields of wheat from which we had received fire. It was here that the next line of Russian defence awaited us, this side of Põltsamaa. I can still see in my mind's eye the white-painted Pilistvere church where we put our signals vehicles under cover, for the Russian artillery had the entire area of our regiment's advance in sight and range. It was our first experience of artillery fire concentrated in such a manner.

In the area around Pilistvere we came to a place on the road of our advance at which three trucks of the advance party had been ambushed. We found the massacred crews in the ditch under the trees to the left of the road – eyes gouged out, sex organs cut off. The corpses were already decomposing. Worms had already moved into the eye sockets and the flesh of the eyebrows. Steel helmets and equipment lay scattered around. The message from the Russians was that they took no prisoners. This included men found wounded who were killed off as unnecessary ballast for the Red Army. The Soviets were not signatories to the Geneva Convention. This fact came home to us here for the first time. Ambulances, recognisable from afar by the large red cross on a white background, seemed to be priority targets.

Now we understood the merciless cruelty of this war. As a result of what we saw here, the conviction spread amongst us all that it was now victory or death. Our fate as soldiers at the front was less important than sparing the people at home such cruelty. In any case a certain black humour now replaced our fear of death to some extent. As for the atrocities which certain German special units committed in the Polish and Russian areas, essentially we knew nothing of them.

In many places the Soviets dug in sections of tree-trunks as anti-tank obstacles.

Põltsamaa

After the Piezai battle the second great milestone for me in the Russian campaign was Põltsamaa where I learned to smoke. Heinz Schimanski and I were ordered to 1st Battalion and on the way to the battalion command post had been forced frequently to leave the highway and seek shelter, the heavy Russian artillery maintaining almost continuous fire on our supply road. In the intervals between each barrage, a few of their 7.62-cm flat-trajectory 'Ratch-Boom' cannons kept up nuisance fire. This was a feared weapon for us because there was absolutely no possibility of reacting to it. The shell arrived and exploded before the sound was heard of the gun discharging. The Russians even used it to fire at a single man. The *Tross* and fighting vehicles strung out across the terrain, and the men of 13th and 14th Companies, all suffered casualties. Gefreiter Heinze of 14th Company, the hero who destroyed ten enemy tanks in twenty minutes at Piezai, fell here. A soldier's fate!

Seizing an opportunity, we had reported to 1st Battalion and then dug a slit trench very quickly, covering it with slivers of tree trunk, brushwood and sods of turf to protect against splinters. At our feet in the trench lay our radio equipment with only the aerial protruding. Hidden thus below ground we felt safer than having to listen to Russian shells whizzing past immediately above our trench. Apparently they suspected that the battalion command post was at the edge of the woods, instead it was about thirty metres beyond in a field of rye. Nevertheless, the concert of shells hissing and bursting tore at the nerves, and then followed the evil spray of sharp shell splinters swirling out from the axis of the explosion to end up in the field or tree trunks. The black smoke would clear – and if one did not hear the cry '*Sanitäter!*' ('Medic') one could be content, though often those hit were no longer able to call out.

The first casualty in our immediate vicinity was the provisions cart. It had been driven up the field path along the edge of the wood, and now its dead horses lay near our slit trench. The heat bloated their bodies and a stinking broth welled up from their wounds. Who could ever forget this stink of carcass, which one came across constantly in these weeks of the advance! Heinz and I left our slit trench only for the most urgent reasons. Our toilet was a shell crater behind the rotting horses. We had to monitor the telephone connection and if this were interrupted then we would superimpose telegraphy so as to guarantee that the battalion was never cut off from the regiment, and that was our job.

One day Heinz offered me his pack of cigarettes with the invitation, 'Go on, take it, it will calm you down.' It was at a time when our sector was being bombarded by the Russian artillery. Over those ten days I became a chain smoker. The cigarette butts which we extinguished in the earth surrounding our slit

A captured Russian field gun and behind it in the roadside ditch the wreckage of a towing unit which to judge by the degree of destruction must have been loaded with ammunition.

trench formed a kind of mosaic, the evidence of a nerve-racked impotence . . .

Those days outside Põltsamaa caused our troops appreciable losses. I remember the shipping out of a seriously wounded man

with blood-soaked bandages, who from the stretcher raised his head slightly, his face waxen and distorted with pain, to cry out, '*Herr Hauptmann*, destroy the Russians – and on to Moscow!' Then his strength gave out and his head sank back.

Our regimental signals platoon also suffered its first losses. Feldwebel Kiausch lost a leg in the churchyard at Pilistvere. At 3rd Battalion a shell exploded on the edge of a slit trench in which three men of the construction troop had sought cover. Horst Salomon, an enthusiastic handball player with the Danzig sporting association, was dead. Shell splinters cut open his body in strips from the legs upward. His two companions, Alois Weiss and Max Herrmann, were seriously wounded. We felt certain they would not be the last. In the Polish and French campaigns our signals platoon had suffered no casualties, even though our regiment had been involved in heavy fighting at Mlava, Pultusk and Praga in Poland, at the storming of Fort Eben Emael in Belgium and at Dunkirk.

After ten days Põltsamaa fell to us almost without a fight. Unteroffizier Presch and Hans Weikert relieved us, and we returned to the regimental command post. We shaved off our beards and washed the filth from our bodies and clothing in a stream. We also did our own laundry until the *Tross* took over the job. Heinz put on face cream and generally made himself very presentable but all was to no avail. Estonia had such beautiful women, but not for front soldiers. The civilians never stayed where there was any shooting.

Oberleutnant von Burgdorf and Leutnant Baltruschat of 151st Infantry Regiment.

Apart from that, there was no time, and no sense in it. The *Etappe* – the rearward services well behind the front – reaped the reward.

I have virtually to gloss over the next few weeks after Põltsamaa. We went this way and that across Estonia, our sweat and filth often mixed in with blood. Once when I had the chance to relax in a cool, mossy glade and consider how wonderful this place would be without warfare I was rudely returned to reality by a shell exploding nearby. One of our 10.5-cm howitzers had fired short, probably too few rings of powder in the cartridge.

Marching could come as a relief. In the summer heat when no danger threatened, the men would remove their steel helmets.

I gained the impression from this incident that German shells had significantly more powerful explosive effect than those of the Russians. Thank heavens, however, this was the only shell which fell short; the rest reached the enemy.

Estonia had become a secondary theatre of war. Strong groups of panzers and motorised units had crossed the Estonian–

A wrecked Russian BT-5 tank being passed by a column of infantry.

Russian frontier and were heading for Leningrad. It was now left to our army corps to wipe out the still powerful enemy forces in Estonia. This task was known in our sector of the front. We had heard the Special Bulletins announcing fantastic successes with thousands of Russian aircraft and tanks destroyed, and millions of prisoners taken in the great encirclements of the central and

southern sectors. Moreover, the total fighting strength of the Russian armies was down to twenty-five divisions. The collapse of Russian resistance seemed only a matter of days or weeks away. And yet we often had the sensation that we had no more reserves. Why otherwise had we been kept in action at the front since 22 June without a single day of rest? This reinforced the impression that our division was the only one present in Estonia, and it had been left to us to do everything.

Sometimes a detachment would lead us off to look for Russian units cut off from their main force. I remember one such exhausting operation near Lake Peipus on the Estonian–Russian frontier: sand, fir trees, scorching heat, hilly country with juniper undergrowth, fields of wheat and marching – marching until we dropped. The reported Russian unit had long since withdrawn. Heinz and I had to send the situation report to the regiment. We sat below some pines, the sands heated by the sun, bathed in sweat and totally exhausted. We were encoding the message: 'Z is I', 'G is S', 'E is L' and I fell asleep. Heinz's sleepy voice awoke me. 'Come on, no sleeping!' The encryption dragged on. Then Heinz fell asleep. We were too exhausted to continue. Finally the operation was called off, and we returned to the regiment.

Rejoining the main body we headed north-west for Reval: in the Wesenberg region our push to the Gulf of Finland had succeeded and split the Russian Front in Estonia. The closer we came to the Estonian capital, the fiercer became the resistance.

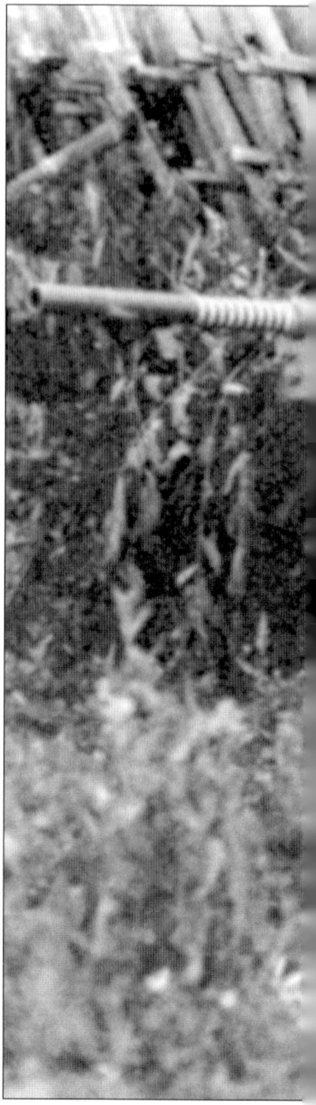

Biplanes,[2] *Rata* fighters and anti-aircraft guns supported the Russian units. Because of the better reception there, mostly we set up our radio equipment in the loft of a farmhouse, and quite frequently one of the aircraft would almost scrape the roof. Once Heinz muttered, 'Man, he could have leaned down and swiped our radio set, the pig was flying so low – but all the same I'm glad not to be Russian – what they have to put up with!' He was right. Those Red Army soldiers we captured were shabby, filthy, unshaven, head hair shaved almost to a stubble. In the jute bag carried on their backs they would have mostly a bit of bread, sugar cut from a sugar loaf, sometimes a scrap of herring. The rest of the bag was for carrying as much infantry ammunition as it would hold. Their appearance was frightful. 'My God, if they let them loose in Germany!' Heinz said. Later our troops captured at Stalingrad looked every bit as bad: exhausted, starving and frozen to the marrow.

In August 1941 we occupied the readiness zones for the offensive against Reval. Narva, the Estonian border town on the river of the same name, had just fallen to the Wehrmacht, and the two divisions released came to join us. Thus we now had 254th Infantry Division to our right and 217th Infantry Division to our left. I remember a street sign which read 'Talinn, 51 kilometres'. Our first reinforcements arrived: Bubi Büchs from Paderborn was a telegraphist, Reimann, Tausch and Krebs brought the telephonists of the regimental signals platoon up to strength. The couple of days until the

The most successful German anti-tank gun of the time, the 3.7-cm, was used in the battle at Piezai/Lithuania from 24 to 26 June 1941. The gun-layer is Gefreiter Paul Heinze.

offensive began we sat at table in the open air and ate fine meals on plates lent by a farmer's wife. This put us in good heart!

The Battle for Reval

On 20 August 1941 our entire front launched its attack on the Soviet-occupied Estonian capital. To support our divisional artillery, we had been allocated a 21-cm mortar and some 8.8-cm flak guns. And aircraft of course.

The Russians had mobilised all the civilian population available for labour to help create fortifications and trench systems and so we knew what to expect: the defence potential would be used to the maximum, especially their anti-aircraft guns, anti-tank guns and tanks for direct fire into our field positions. This would present us with a major difficulty: the Russians had dug in the tanks up to their turrets, providing them with a huge field of fire while leaving us little to aim at.

On the first day of the offensive we came to a place where our 161st Reconnaissance Battalion, coming from a minor road into the main highway, had encountered a convoy of Russian trucks flowing back. Our anti-tank guns had opened fire at once destroying people and materials. A ghastly scene met our eyes. Amongst the scorched, literally roasted Russian soldiers was a girl, probably a nurse. She lay naked, all her clothing having been burnt from her body, her legs angled to one side, a flat British steel helmet on her head and she had defecated, evidently the anal sphincter had abandoned its function with the onset of her death. This is one of the terrible images which imprinted itself indelibly in my memory and I have never been able to forget it ever since.

Our radio team had been ordered to 1st Battalion. It was drizzling. After a change of position we had set up our equipment in a peat-cutting strip behind bricks set up for drying the peat. From here we had established contact with the regiment.

'What, you're connected to the regiment?' the officer asked. 'Can I reach the 21-cm mortar firing position through them?' The enquirer was the advanced spotter for the mortar but was cut off from the battery. We got to work and once we had tapped out the encoded data to our regiment, it was less than ten minutes before the heavy projectiles roared away above us and reached their target, the armoured fortifications in the yard of a cellulose factory and the Reval airfield. A gigantic explosion in the factory was followed by the blossoming of a large black cloud of smoke. The rain stopped and now we had fine weather.

In the course of the next few days we advanced to the area of the old German First World War fortifications; some large grey concrete bunkers. The communication trenches had decayed and were overgrown with grasses, but they provided sufficient cover for an infantryman ducking low. The dangerous spots of these old German defensive installations were the occasional breaks in the lines of trenches at which the dug-in Russian tanks and anti-tank guns were zeroed-in. Although their trajectories were too flat to land in the trenches, those shells which exploded at the trench edges were dangerous enough. It was a tremendous relief to achieve the unavoidable sprint across the open strips. After making sure I still had all body parts intact, I would repair at once to the old concrete bunkers where protection was guaranteed.

The sound of battle grew in intensity and white puffs of exploding AA shells dotted the blue sky in their hundreds. Quite high above the haze I made out a flight of our bombers, either Heinkel 111s or Junkers 88s, but the concentrated AA fire probably made aimed bombing impossible. The Russians were shooting from hundreds of AA guns of all calibres. The assembly of shipping inside and off Reval harbour was spared by our bombers. In the entire Russian campaign I never saw anti-aircraft batteries on this scale again. Soon Soviet naval gunnery from offshore also joined in.

The number of prisoners we took mounted daily. Many Soviet soldiers came to us with hands raised calling, '*Nyet Ruski – Ukrainski*' in the hope of obtaining preferential treatment as Ukrainians – certainly leaflets dropped over enemy lines promised

German infantry after their first experience of contact with the enemy.

them this. In war, any means is justified to weaken the enemy – empty promises! On our way to the new battalion command post we came across two Estonian girls in Russian uniforms wearing flat British steel helmets and a first-aid box around their necks. We had a closer look at this curiosity, girls serving with the infantry, Heinz with an ironical smile of derision. One of them gave us a stare both fearful and hostile. She was expecting to be killed or at least raped at any moment for which the corresponding Russian propaganda would undoubtedly have prepared her. Since nothing of the kind happened and Heinz offered her a German cigarette, the courageously suppressed fear regarding the evil *Germanski* soldiers evaporated visibly. Lying propaganda – and in general it always is – stirs people to hatred and is the basis for much cruelty in war.

I did not know until much later of the miserable existence which faced the greater mass of Russian prisoners in German hands, treatment quite different to that which the British, French and later the Americans went through, but fairly similar to the treatment meted out by the Soviets to their German prisoners post-war, as I was to experience subsequently at first hand.

Our new battalion command post was located in a small single-floor wooden farmhouse in which the only solid item was a brick-built stove. Heinz and I were in the garden digging a slit trench when a great shell-burst rocked the house, followed by splinters, then dust and powder-smoke forced out through the windows. An armour-piercing shell had passed through the house wall and exploded against the oven. Pale but uninjured, those inside, who included officers, beat a hasty retreat into the garden to seek protection with us. Next day we moved to a fresh position. During this procedure the Russians announced their arrival from thick woodland behind us with shouts of '*Urra!*'

'The Russians are attacking! Everybody in position!'

I thrust off the radio pack from my shoulders, loaded a magazine into the carbine, one round in the breech and then I threw myself

Oberst Walter Melzer, Commanding Officer, 151st Infantry Regiment (standing), and his Signals Officer, Leutnant Dr Hubatsch.

German infantry advancing and expecting contact with the enemy, therefore wearing steel helmets on the march.

down into a depression in the ground. The Russian infantry came from our rear firing and shouting '*Urra!*' and were quickly shelled by our 10.5-cm howitzers. Now we saw what they wanted. Russian stragglers knew the position of one of our batteries and were intent on capturing it. All barrels were turned on them and in the welter of direct fire their undertaking collapsed. Soon a deathly

hush fell – the stillness of the cemetery! I had not needed to shoot, thank goodness, and this was actually the first time I had had to exchange my radio equipment for a rifle.

We took over the Reval lighthouse. It had thick, sturdy walls and despite being under constant fire from Russian naval guns we felt absolutely safe there. From the room at the top one could observe the port and far out over the Baltic. We counted more than sixty Russian ships, mainly troop transports and escort vessels, amongst them the cruiser *Kirov*.

Next day, 28 August 1941, we signals men were issued with hand grenades 'which might be needed for house-to-house fighting'. I put a stick grenade in my belt and another in the shaft of my boot. This seemed a very dangerous development. With sleeves rolled up we marched off. The expected strong enemy resistance, present during the last few days, appeared to have evaporated, however. Almost unnoticed we got ever closer to the city centre. At 1330 hrs the Nazi war flag was hoisted on city hall.

In the foyer of the building Heinz and I met members of the 2nd Battalion signals staff. We left our equipment on a table. Outside in the square the Estonian townspeople were celebrating their liberation exuberantly, and treated our troops with the greatest cordiality. The companies of the regiment formed up for the official entry into the city; it made an impressive picture, this triumphal march of the victors of the battle. Oberleutnant Zonewitz marched at the head of his company wearing his somewhat battered peaked cap, his sun-tanned, strikingly manly face as dusty as his boots. He was the perfect picture of the infantry officer and warrior for the Fatherland. I was seized by the conquering spirit. While Estonian men in open trucks drove through the city waving national flags, we sent friendly, encouraging looks towards the Estonian girls at the wayside and one could often hear the words '*Illus saksa boys!*' ('Good-looking German boys!') being shouted back. But what advantage could we take of it, we who were going to have to pull out again before nightfall?

A woman in her mid-thirties came to us in the city hall with large plates of sandwiches and repeated over and over her gratitude that we had freed Estonia from the Russians. She spoke good German. A soldier called Knebel from 2nd Battalion, a Saxon, could not resist saying; 'You would have preferred having the British here instead of the Germans, wouldn't you?' There was a short embarrassed pause and then the lady said, 'Well yes, since you ask, I would have. But we are so grateful to you for having rid us of that ghastly Communist hegemony.' The banter continued for a while in the same vein, but did nothing to impair the basically joyous mood.

We moved out the same evening, probably through Baltischport, but wherever it was we never spent a single night in Reval. At Lihula, a small town a little north of Riga Bay we were billeted in clean wooden houses and thought that for us the war was now over, or that at worst we would be just a security force at the coast. In fact this was what was on the agenda if the campaign had gone as planned, but soon a divisional order of the day put us right: 'My soldiers! Unfortunately I cannot yet grant you your long deserved rest, for a small but important task has to be performed first . . .' and so on. This understatement meant we had to occupy the Baltic Islands, whatever *they* were, and as to whose existence I had been unaware until that moment. And the bad news was, we had to eject the Russians from them.

Chapter 3 Notes

1. On 11 August 1920 under the Latvian–Soviet Peace Treaty, Bolshevik Russia relinquished all claims to Latvian territory. At the outbreak of war in September 1939, Latvia declared its neutrality but under the Molotov–Ribbentrop Pact the Nazis and Soviets secretly agreed that Latvia fell into the Soviet sphere of interest. On 16 June 1940 the Soviet Union invaded Latvia and annexed it. Many Latvians welcomed the arrival of the Germans in 1941. *Trans.*
2. The author probably means the Polikarpov I-153 *Chaika* fighter. *Trans.*

CHAPTER 4

Operation Beowulf

Beowulf was an amphibious operation and offensive carried out by the German Army and Kriegsmarine in the late summer of 1941. It was designed to eject Soviet forces occupying the offshore islands of Moon, Ösel and Dagö, the last foothold of the Russians in Estonia. The Kriegsmarine would carry out landings on the west and south-east coast of Ösel and on the north coast of Dagö to divert attention from the movement of Army troops across the Sound of Moon. On 13 September the 3rd S-boat Flotilla with torpedo boats, minesweepers, R-boats, minelayers and smaller craft was in position and at readiness.

IT WAS ON 13 SEPTEMBER 1941 that we folded up our tents at Lihula and then checked over the radio equipment. The two-man teams attached to 1st and 2nd Battalions, 151st Infantry Regiment, were given an extra man as reserve in case of any losses in combat, this third man also had to carry reserve power sources such as lead collectors and anode batteries. Schimanski, our third man Fritz Krebs, and I remained at the regimental command post this time because our last operation before Reval had been with 1st Battalion.

Our readiness area was directly facing the island of Moon, about ten kilometres out in the Baltic. Its terrain was flat, mainly woods, marsh and fields, the highest point above sea level being sixty-eight metres. Ninety assault boats lay ready to ship the first wave across. On the way 'forward' we saw in our artillery position many of the guns which our division normally lacked, ranging from collapsible mountain guns planned for the initial direct support of the infantry landings to 21-cm guns.

Infantry of 61st Infantry Division advancing through a field of corn in Latvia.

We had fine autumnal weather, but the nights were drawing in and cool. The countryside around us was unwooded and strewn with large stones and boulders of all sizes with juniper groves

between. Night fell, the sea was almost calm; from the shore we heard only ripples and waves lapping against rocks. On the enemy-held littoral of the island of Moon searchlights installed at regular distances swept the waters. The first hours of 14 September 1941 passed, the dew was settling and I felt cold. I wrapped myself in a blanket.

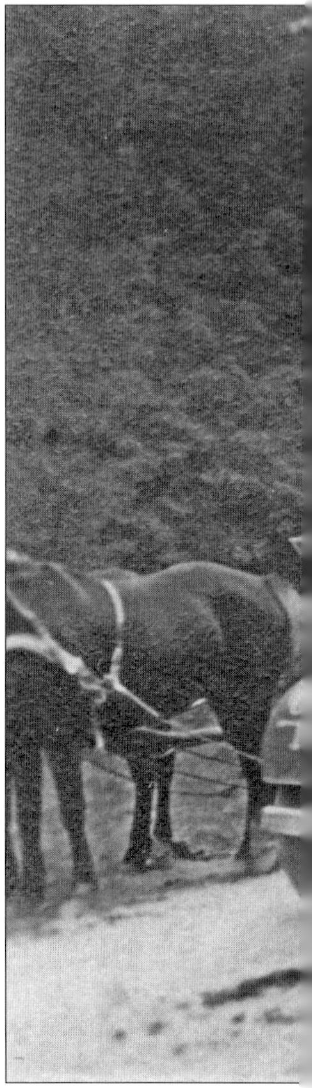

At 0400 hrs precisely every German artillery piece along the coast stabbed flame sending shells roaring across the water to the island. The noise was tremendous. In the skyglow one could see our gunners working hard at reloading. The assault boats carrying the men of 1st Battalion and its radio troop had been at sea since long before this sudden artillery barrage. Ever the optimist, I told myself that since there was only a single battalion of Russians on Ösel it shouldn't be so bad. Taking into account the preparations I had seen being made for our attack it should have been obvious to me that it did not require a reinforced infantry division and additional field guns to wipe out a battalion of Russians. The assurances we had been given! Did we need to be deceived? Even in the later course of the war they treated us as idiots, and we believed and trusted them blindly, controlled by wishful thinking.

From along the banks of the shore a machine gun chattered and then fell silent. The assault boats with the first companies aboard got lost in the dark and arrived back at the landing stage thinking they were on Moon before realising their error. Heinz Schimanski and I sat at the radio equipment, headphones on, waiting anxiously for the first sign of life from our opposite numbers at 1st Battalion. Our frequency was silent. We sent our call sign at regular intervals but received no response. An hour passed – still silence. We began to be concerned: only ten kilometres across the sea, we had seven aerials up and water is

General Siegfried Haenicke, commanding officer of 61st Infantry Division, standing in his staff car passing a horse-drawn supply column of his division, Latvia, July 1941.

a good conductor, so how could our equipment be insufficient for the distance? Gloomier thoughts crept into our deliberations. Perhaps the radio troop had drowned. The men of the battalion

A light armoured troop-carrier half-track of a temporarily attached neighbouring panzer unit, Latvia, July 1941. Unlike infantry divisions like the 61st, the infantry included in panzer divisions were motorised.

would not know our frequency or call sign. If the water had been deeper than reported at the disembarkation point and the radio equipment or batteries were submerged, that might also account for it.

Two hours had now passed since the assault boats had set out across the Sound of Moon. Finally, clear and sharp as if the transmitter were only 500 metres away, the morsed message came through our headphones. Heinz copied down the encoded text, asked the sender to wait, checked that the groups were of five letters each and then confirmed receipt. The message was now decoded in the presence of the platoon commander, Leutnant Hubatsch, who could scarcely contain his impatience. Now we had the story. The boats had landed two kilometres to the south of where intended, and directly in front of the enemy base at the village of Kuivastu. They had encountered heavy resistance and were bogged down.

This first signal, tapped out by Pat Wachnowski at 0550 hrs, enabled the regiment to take action. Holding a small and narrow bridgehead meant a defensive struggle, which brought their very survival into question. Shortly after the numbers were increased by the arrival of Oberleutnant Baltruschat and his company. The enemy had recovered from their surprise and were also taking increased defensive measures.

It had grown light by the time when the second wave with 2nd Battalion motored out for Kuivastu. Russian biplanes, circling over the sea between the mainland and the island, strafed the assault boats with their machine guns. Whoever escaped the attentions of the aircraft ran into the very effective field of fire of the anti-aircraft and anti-tank guns ashore. Water fountains sprayed up:

Vehicles of the 61st Division staff, Latvia, 1941.

The Commanding Officer of 1st Battalion, 162nd Infantry Regiment, Major Gottfried Weber (*right*), in conversation with two of his company commanders.

a number of assault boats literally reared up from the water before breaking apart. From near the foreshore enemy machine guns and 12.2-cm heavy mortars, our first experience of the latter weapon, added to the problem.

The losses of assault boats and the men of the second wave aboard them were grievous. They had been exposed in full daylight to the defenders without any possibility of cover, and these serious losses occurred while still on the water. Whole crews sank dead or wounded in the waves. 2nd Battalion Commanding Officer Oberstleutnant Driedger received severe stomach wounds. Those men who remained able-bodied jettisoned their heavy equipment and clothing and swam towards one of the small islands near Moon. Lifejackets had been issued for the operation and these saved many lives here.

In this situation the Luftwaffe came to the rescue. The Messerschmitt Bf 109s made a clean sweep of the biplanes and our Ju 88s created havoc for the field fortifications. As if on an exercise, they headed for the target, pitched down on an oblique flight-path, released their bomb loads and regained altitude at the same kind of angle. Meanwhile other machines of the flight awaited their turn to attack a different target. Bombs burst, the beams of the fortifications flew through the air and mushroom-shaped smoke clouds climbed high. The job, made to measure for the Ju 88s, enabled the bridgehead to be enlarged decisively. Without the air support, the small group in the Moon bridgehead would not have come through it. Pat Wachnowski could now bring out his radio equipment from behind the cemetery wall which had provided him with cover against Russian rifle fire. He did not think he could have held out very much longer before they reached him.

The situation for our troops on Moon had stabilised, and the regiment on the mainland changed its position. In the third wave we of the radio team had an assault boat to ourselves. Wearing steel helmets and crouching low in the bow we set off. The motor howled and the coxswain in the stern stood staring ahead, his hands behind him controlling the outboard. From where I squatted this looked very impressive. The assault boats were the shape of an elongated canoe with thwarts and no more than five metres in length. The sea was no longer calm and a swell lifted the bow: when it dropped water splashed on board. Our faces were dripping and we looked adventurous and sporting. Heinz and I looked at each other and laughed. It was fun, this short sea crossing – but not for long. More Russian biplanes appeared, showed interest and were just preparing to dive down on the main group of boats astern of us when Bf 109s came suddenly into view making the biplanes turn away surprisingly quickly.

The enemy's anti-aircraft and anti-tank guns were not so accurate as they had been for the second wave. The projectiles hissed over our heads and exploded in the sea far to our rear. We saw infantrymen swimming for their lives, all heading for a small island to the right that had trees and shrubbery offering good cover. Lightly wounded 'shipwreck survivors' clung grimly to the floating remains of assault boats until rescue boats arrived to fish them out. As we approached the shore our own boat made a sharp turn, the sign for us to disembark, and then the coxswain took it back to the Estonian mainland. I found myself knee-deep in sea water, holding the radio equipment above water by the handle. I stumbled on the rough gravel bottom and dropped the carrying strap. The strap was essential and I fished around for it in the murky water stirred up by the sand. There was a spray of water. I forgot the strap and hurried ashore. A sniper in a tree had had me in his sights – and fired one metre too short. Then I remembered that I had spare jute carrying straps in the accessories pack.

The radio team met up ashore, hidden from the view of snipers, and we had a breathing space to organise. First we made an open fire for drying our clothing and watched our landings continue uninterrupted without enemy interference. Siebel ferries[1] had now begun bringing trucks, heavy equipment and artillery to the island. Heinz and I found a haystack for the night which we had to share with infantry from other units. During the night my Agfa-Isolette camera disappeared.

This was the prelude to the battle for the strategically important Baltic Islands. It was a daring operation to use on the open sea assault boats designed and built for crossing rivers and lakes. It was a first for the German Wehrmacht and it worked. Within two days we had almost cleared the 200-square kilometre island of Moon.

Onwards into Ösel and Dagö

Only from the visually impenetrable scrubland on the Moon side of the Ösel causeway were the Russians able to halt the advance of our 1st and 2nd Battalions. This action cost many more brave German soldiers their lives. Finally, when we had our backs free, we crossed the causeway. Put like that it sounds simple but in reality it was rated as a difficult operation probably with high casualties, something for which Führer-HQ had let it be known that the successful commander would likely earn the Knight's Cross.

The causeway, 3.6 kilometres long and still extant today, connected the island of Moon with the main offshore island of Ösel. The causeway was ruler-straight, as wide as a road, lined with railings on either side and was made from earth, broken rocks and stone. Unquestionably practical in peacetime, it offered no cover for an advancing force of soldiers, who would have to be favoured by fortune if the transit was to be made without very serious casualties. Hauptmann Pankow, former commander of our HQ Company and deputising for the seriously wounded Oberstleutnant Driedger, decided to take 7th Company, 2nd Battalion, across the causeway. Although it had been blown up at several places along its length by the retreating Russians, the gaps provided certain possibilities of cover. Much more important was the enemy's failure to establish an effective defence at the far end. A few machine guns and anti-tank guns suitably placed there

would have inflicted very heavy casualties as is easily imagined. However, our brave Ju 88s and Bf 109s showed up again and the fighters set about the Russian biplanes harassing our troops on the causeway. A fair number of the Soviet biplanes tipped forward after receiving bursts of fire and, trailing smoke, plunged into the sea. When the waves flattened and the smoke cleared they had left no trace.

The Ju 88s' tactics forced everybody on the far shore and in the village of Orissaare to take cover. After air reconnaissance reported while flags in the village, in the afternoon the regiment marched across in a long column. Prisoners then repaired the damaged sections and made the dam passable for traffic. A long file of Russians captured on Ösel by the advanced battalions, amongst them many officers up to the rank of colonel, were led across the causeway into Moon. I found a portable gramophone and Russian records in an abandoned shelter, and so had something to replace my guitar which had come apart before Reval due to rain damage.

Orissaare was still within range of the Russian artillery but our bridgehead had been expanded considerably. Everything went off with precision, above all the cooperation between Army and Luftwaffe was exemplary. Our radio troop (Schimanski and I) was attached again to 1st Battalion. We heard that in the north of the island an airborne landing by a

A grave for two German soldiers of 61st Infantry Division

special unit of the Brandenburgers, who had the task of silencing the shore batteries, had not gone well and few had survived.

1st Battalion advanced smartly to the south-west through the centre section of the island. Ninety kilometres long and fifty kilometres wide, much of it was flat land overgrown with juniper and strewn with light-coloured boulders. The people lived from fishing; agricultural cultivation could not have amounted to much and farming was limited to cattle. In glorious autumn weather we found the island beautiful.

On 20 September we reached the area around Arensburg, the island capital. Air reconnaissance reported that Arensburg had raised the white flag and was probably expecting us. Next morning the regiment sent trucks in order that we should reach it more quickly than by marching. The road into the town was slightly downhill so that we could see it clearly on the southern horizon. Suddenly the sound of the rustling wind was mixed with a familiar evil chirping, the brakes squealed and with leaps and bounds we dived into the cover of a roadside ditch.

Immediately before the entrance to the town the Russians had set up a well-developed and camouflaged interception position which greeted us with heavy machine-gun and mortar fire. Our infantry companies found it difficult to identify the enemy's exact location and had to resort to knocking out one machine-gun nest after another while we waited for the all-clear in the ditch. Above us on the road were the remains of a couple of VW amphibious cars, which belonged to the paymaster and his entourage who were travelling with us. These people had very long faces, not being accustomed to being shot at. Their grandchildren would certainly hear all about what they had had to go through! I exchanged a malicious grin with Schimanski. They had assumed that Arensburg would be free of the enemy. What booty they expected to find in the town I was unable to establish.

Finally the resistance was broken down and we approached the town on foot. Our mood was by then more subdued for having seen the German dead lying in the meadows. Some looked as though death had surprised them suddenly, others were covered over with a cape, only the boots being visible. Nothing moved: no arms, no groans, nothing – dead. A soft breeze from the sea played in their hair, in the hair of those who but an hour ago had been full of life; now everything was ended. Their staring eyes perceived nothing, the transition into the realm of the dead was complete. Their bodies cooled, stiffened in rigor, loosened and then decomposed before they had really begun to live their lives. The dead would know nothing of the tears their mothers would shed for them. They would never be forgotten, but only by those who loved them. The Fatherland? No, the official Fatherland of the future would be more likely to disavow them, ashamed of its war dead. That is the sad truth.

Arensburg, a small town of narrow, cobble-stone streets and mainly wooden houses welcomed us. The extraordinary great fortress built by the Teutonic Knights in the late fourteenth century towered over the roofs of the low houses. The town had been spared apart from a few dwellings on the periphery. For our regiment the battle for Ösel had terminated, or so we thought. It was left to the 162nd Infantry Regiment (from our 61st Division) to 'cleanse' the long Sworbe peninsula jutting into the Gulf of Riga to where the Russians had retreated.

Our quarters lay a little outside of the town. Oberst Melzer, awarded the Knight's Cross for his actions at Reval, had fulfilled his duties in battle and could now grant his soldiers their long-deserved rest. Heinz and I were returned to the regimental signals platoon. It was such a pleasure to be able to wash and shave in peace. Then we fetched out the portable gramophone and listened to Russian records, all of good quality, mostly folk songs with soloist and choir: melancholy mixed with wildness.

Our enjoyment of the quiet days excused duty was soon clouded. We began increasingly to hear the sound of battle from the distant front. The artillery fire grew heavier day by day. In

Time to reflect at the graveside of their comrade
Gefreiter Gerhard Grewe of 7th Company,
162nd Infantry Regiment, who fell on 29 July 1941.

between one could make out distinctly the heavy fortress guns shooting at Abruka, a small island still held by the Soviets. It gave us an uneasy feeling and misgivings, and these did not lie.

After our week's grace we had to relieve the battered 162nd. They had made no progress forwards and many had bled to death before the Soviets' earth bunkers. The defensive lines were deeply staggered on the entire peninsula with a network of communicating trenches. Heinz and I were attached to 3rd Battalion. The worst of the fighting on Ösel was now before us.

The Sworbe peninsula is several kilometres long and connected to the island of Ösel by an isthmus two kilometres wide. There were two coastal roads, one for going west, the other east. The Soviet artillery at Abruka had zeroed in on these two roads, and even by night subjected them to nuisance fire. We passed along them for our departure position, the earth, and not only the earth, trembling at the explosions.

On one of the last days of September 1941 our attack began. We were always crossing territory which had been mined. The Russian anti-personnel mines were laid in wooden boxes to avoid detection by our equipment. Therefore we moved on tiptoe, or in any case very cautiously, as if on eggshells, until we reached firm ground which if possible had been trodden previously. The civilian population here had had much to suffer, Every village had gone up in flames and no house was left intact; only the brick-built chimneys were left standing among the ashes and rubble. The inhabitants had fled into the woods and lived there as primitives. Even here the war touched them and many lost their lives.

We arrived at Anseküla to find that the resistance had stiffened, and the enemy had to be winkled out again bunker by bunker assisted by 161st Pioneer Battalion with its squads of flamethrowers. A recognised enemy position would be subdued with machine-gun fire and then the bunker taken with the flamethrower, balled charges and hand grenades until the living torches tumbled out into the open and the rest surrendered.

Sturmgeschütz III self-propelled assault guns accompanying the advance of 61st Infantry Division troops.

Gefreiter Schulz from Litzmannstadt won the Knight's Cross.[2] His daring was almost incredible because he always emerged as the victor and was never wounded. Acting alone, he cleaned out

bunker after bunker. He was so possessed that he would even keep going when his flamethrower was shot to pieces. Then he would roll in the grass to extinguish the flames on his burning clothing, get up and attack the bunker with his pistol and demolition charges only – always successfully. Schulz was sent to the rearward *Tross* by his battalion commanding officer in order that this valuable man should not be lost to to us too soon. There actually are heroes to whom it does not matter that they are heroes, but in the long run no infantryman can avoid being killed, wounded or being taken prisoner. There are no alternatives but some heroes are the glorious exception.

Our attack was supported increasingly by the Luftwaffe and above all the artillery. There was the following strange experience at an important crossroads held by strong Russian forces that had to be softened up prior to our assault The regiment ordered that a particular line must be held while we waited for a barrage by all our artillery at 1300 hrs. Our notorious 3rd Battalion under Hauptmann Rooch had apparently crossed the line, whether intentionally or not I never discovered. Heinz and I had set up our radio equipment 100 to 150 metres behind the foremost line. This was in a piece of fir forest such as was rare on Ösel.

Heinz, anticipating the barrage, had just expressed his usual emotions pitying the Russians for what they were about to receive when our guns all fired. The barrage was so massive that I only saw its like again during the war on one other occasion, during the defensive fighting at Lake Ladoga. The shells passed above our heads and exploded very close in an unbelievable inferno of noise. In a split-second we recognised and reacted to the situation. Either they had fired too short or the battalion had moved too far forward. I tore out the power cable and disengaged the equipment before sprinting to the rear. In my haste I got entangled in a bush with the dangling cable. A jolt, I got frcc and kept going. At that moment Oberleutnant Wippern of the battalion staff came running up – we called him 'Fieseler Storch' on account of his long legs – and shouted, 'You, radio man, send; "Barrage on our own lines!"' By the time we had set up the equipment again and re-established contact, the barrage was over. 'My God, there will be men dead, and by their own artillery!' I thought. Nothing of the kind! The battalion did not even have a man wounded.

The barrage fell exactly halfway between the companies and the battalion command post. The battalion staff fled to the rear, and the companies fled ahead, and the Russians ran ahead of the companies. Much effort, no results – but the barrage had not been unsuccessful for the Russians abandoned the crossroads in the manner described and so the objective had been achieved.

The attack proceeded. We had left the village of Vitri behind us. It was 3 October 1941. The Russian resistance still appeared to be unbroken but collapsed next day, first in small groups and then they came towards us in endless streams, officers riding small horses, their boots almost scraping the ground. These riders were an odd sight. The battle for Ösel was over. Some of their officers took their own lives, either by priming a hand grenade and holding it against their chests, or by a bullet through the head. The calls for reinforcements they had radioed had been ignored. All calls to Moscow for help had gone unanswered. Where would such help have come from anyway?

Our wireless monitoring team had been listening in to their pleas, and then heard them give up trying. Towards midday we reached the southern tip of the peninsula by the lighthouse. A fat black-haired cook at a Russian field kitchen served Russian tinned foods to German soldiers. He pressed me to try some. I did so unwillingly but his spicy beef was first class, tinned with bay leaf and peppercorn. Our insipid equivalent could not compete.

I have forgotten the name of the small village near the lighthouse on the southernmost tip of Sworbe.[3] In the small wooden Evangelical church, German soldiers began arriving straight from the front, sweating and covered in dust, stick grenades in their belts and in the shafts of their boots, the sleeves of their tunics rolled up, steel helmets removed. The vicar's wife, whose husband had been deported to Russia, delivered a sermon in which she told the congregation of the Estonian people's suffering at the hands of the Soviets. Many of the German soldiers there were Catholics from the Rhineland and Westphalia, but the fact that the church was of the Protestant confession was irrelevant.

The battle for Ösel had ended. Eleven thousand Russian prisoners were taken, hundreds of field guns, armoured vehicles, trucks, machine guns and huge quantities of equipment had fallen into the hands of the Wehrmacht. It was obvious that a Russian battalion could not have been here all by itself; at the very least there was a division. Having returned to Arensburg we were now ordered to prepare for the final operation in the Estonian Baltic Islands, namely to evict Russian troops on Dagö, the second-largest of the islands which lies north of Ösel. This was not a very difficult task for our division, for our 176th Infantry Regiment had already gone in before us. These operations had been carried out in the early hours of 12 October and had not been met with much resistance.

Towards midday our regiment crossed the Soela Sound in assault boats; apparently the landings would not be safe any other way. The good weather held, however, and we were not molested while at sea; we were disembarked directly into the water as

The graves of two men of 1st Battalion, 162nd Infantry Regiment, who fell in the summer of 1941.

before and waded ashore. The first job was to dry our uniforms, for which purpose large fires were lit; that night brought the first frost and a light snowfall that did not persist beyond sunrise. The days that followed were quiet from my point of view; it does not mean that our regiment was not involved in heavy fighting in other sectors. In fact, the regimental commander decided to form a small advanced unit composed of 7th Company under Leutnant Krüger and 'a radio troop' from the regimental signals platoon to maintain contact with Leutnant Hubatsch. Schimanski led the 'radio troop' which consisted of himself and me.

I had misgivings about being part of an advance party. We headed for Kärdla, the principal village in the north of the island, 'creeping' in our motor vehicles through thick woodland along field paths. We spent the night in the house of the forester. Even to me, a mere *Gefreiter*, this operation seemed to lack any sense since if we were to make any kind of contact with the enemy it would be from his ambush. We reached Kärdla without incident, however. Nearby the Russians had a heavy coastal battery which kept pounding the Tahkuna peninsula and surrounding territory fairly constantly. I spent the night in a house whose window panes rattled alarmingly at every exploding shell. The night was cold with snow flurries but at least I had a roof over my head whereas our infantry had none. Winter had begun.

In the attack next morning the Russian defensive lines gave way and they pulled back to the Tahkuna peninsula to make their last stand. By the following morning they had lost the will to fight just as their division on Sworbe had done, but here on a much smaller scale. The battle for the Baltic Islands was therefore concluded.

Next day was 21 October 1941 and we returned to Ösel by Siebel ferry. There we were informed that we were not to be the occupying force for the Baltic Islands but form part of Eighteenth Army as its operational reserve attached to Army Group North. Our division had to assemble at the River Narva and we set off without further ado. It was a few days' march along Estonia's northern coastal road bordering the Gulf of Finland, spending the nights in warm Estonian homes which all had a natural cosiness. Optimism and faith in the outcome were mandatory and so we marched towards victory. For us Sudeten Germans there could be no alternative, for if we lost the war we could expect a bloodbath at the hands of the Czechs. So, don't think about it, just trust in the *Führer*!

Narva appeared ghostlike before us from the mist and darkness, dominated by the two massive fortresses built in the Middle Ages, symbolising the meeting place of two cultures: the four-cornered tower of the Hermannsfeste on the west bank of the river, and the great rounded turret of the Ivangorod fortress on its east bank. We were billeted for two days in the Hermannsfeste, lit internally by miserable oil lamps. Here at Narva, Feldwebel Hofer from Tilsit joined the regimental signals platoon and took over as platoon sergeant for a while.

Chapter 4 Notes

1. Siebel ferries were shallow-draft catamaran landing craft. The Siebelfähre 40 for example had two 500-hp V-8 motors and three BMW 300-hp aircraft engines which provided maximum speeds of 11 km/hr, or 14 km/hr using all five engines. Dimensions: 21.6 m. long × 13.9 m. wide and 1.2 m. maximum draft loaded. The maximum loading was 60 tonnes or 150 men. *Trans.*
2. This was Gefreiter Heinrich Schulz of 3rd Company, 161st Pioneer Battalion. He was awarded the Knight's Cross on 18 October 1941. *Trans.*
3. The square stone lighthouse which the author mentions was built in 1770 and destroyed during the fighting in 1944. The nearest settlement was Torgu parish. *Trans.*

CHAPTER 5

The Battle of Tikhvin

The Wehrmacht High Command decided that the decisive battles should be fought on all fronts before the onset of winter. The siege of Leningrad was effective as from 8 September 1941. On 16 October 1941 the German Army began its offensive across the Volkhov River with the objective of capturing the town of Tikhvin, 200 kilometres east of Leningrad. From there it was planned that Eighteenth Army would advance to join with the Finns at the Svir River and so complete the encirclement of Leningrad. Tikhvin fell to the Germans on 10 November 1941.

WALTHER HUBATSCH, former Chief of Signals, 151st Grenadier Regiment, wrote of this period in his history of 61st Infantry Division: 'The winter put a premature end to the operations, which had started late; in the second half of November the enemy pressure on this far-advanced position became increasingly strong. The fighting took place in extensive swamps and bottomless morass which frustrated every operation by motorised units. Organisation Todt had built a narrow supply road ['*Rollbahn*'] which could only be used by traffic in one direction. Panzers tended to slip off this log road to right or left and would then sink ever deeper into thick mud.'

That was the situation when our division was required to go to the aid of panzer units involved in heavy fighting in the Tikhvin area. The situation had become so critical that the battalions of our regiment had to be flown there by Ju 52s. The regimental staff followed with the motorised elements of the regiment. Our signals platoon sat with 14th Company on the small open towing

The city limits of the Latvian capital Riga.

vehicles for our 3.7-cm anti-tank guns. Temperatures had fallen to –20 °C so that we had to muffle up with blankets for the ride into the bitter wind. Our route took us through Chudevo from where it was still another 130 kilometres north-east to Tikhvin, always crossing swamps, passing elongated settlements wrapped in winter. Swamps between the Volkhov River and Lake Ladoga extended north-east interspersed with islands of sand and earth, large and small, with settlements. The inhabitants lived on what the poor soil provided while the woodlands must have helped make a source of income possible for a meagre existence.

North-east of the Volkhov the settlements we passed were villages of typical north Russian huts; beam laid upon beam, the gaps sealed with moss and mud, all under a shingle roof. Wooden stairs led up to the living quarters on a raised ground floor. The space between the roof and the living room ceiling was used to store hay and items of equipment. The very important cellar room had to be frost-free and would accordingly be pretty deep in the ground, reached through a trap door in the floor of the living room. Provisions such as potatoes, cabbage and green tomatoes were kept there. Old newspapers were used for wallpaper; wherever these were not available the walls were left in their natural condition with the beams exposed. In the gaps countless cockroaches and bugs would find their home. The most important appointment in the house was the brick oven into which pots were placed for preparing soup. The whole family would sleep on top of the oven. It and the cellar were therefore the most indispensable fixtures of such a Russian house.

A child's cot or bed would be hung suspended by four ropes from a hook at the end of a stake held in place by an iron ring in the ceiling of the living room. A line would dangle from the cot to the mother's position in the bed by which she could gently rock the cradle; it was said that tiny Russians began their training as paratroopers by this method. All these fixtures and fittings were simple but always practical. Characteristic of every village was the

KONDITOREJ
AUGLU TIRGOTA

Sporadic resistance flared up at Riga. Here an abandoned T-26 Russian tank is seen on a road outside a fruit market.

draw-well. The well would have a waist-high square surround of cut logs. There would be a tall, upright forked stave at its head to hold a movable pole with a weight at the short end and a bucket at the other for taking water. Such a village would have a wretched but also often romantic look about it. Its huts were now highly desirable in winter, offering protection against the increasing cold. The local women wore frayed clothes stuffed with wadding over old frocks, and headscarves. Two rugged fur boots would protrude below this attire, practical as was everything else here. The Russians are the unsurpassed masters of improvisation, yet what a contrast to the Baltic States! It seemed to us that we had left civilisation behind when we crossed the Narva. A quite different, hostile, strange and inhospitable territory received us with its numbing winter swamp countryside.

This swampy terrain was the great danger for our advancing units. The line of advance was 130 kilometres long, and because the swamps on either side had frozen and were passable, these open flanks had to be protected. Cobblers, tailors and all other personnel who could possibly be spared by the *Tross* were used as infantry to keep open the supply road to the troops fighting at Tikhvin.

Chilled to the bone, one early afternoon it was already growing dark when we reached a village to spend the night. A haze was rising straight as a candle from the chimneys, mixed with a little smoke, a result of warmed and cold air combining, a common sight in Russian winters. We were distributed amongst

Men of 162nd Infantry Regiment entering Riga city centre.

the village houses. I entered a dark room with several others, the only light coming from the oven hole. Three panzer men had made themselves comfortable here, their upper bodies inclined towards the heat, eyes staring fixedly at the glow. 'Where have you come from?' one of them asked finally. When we supplied the information and announced our destination they lost interest and turned back to the fire. 'Tikhvin? That's a hellish place.'

The room fell quiet except for the crackling of the wood fire in the stove. Once our eyes had grown accustomed to the gloom we noticed the presence of some Russian civilians lying on top of the oven, only feet and clothing visible. We readied ourselves for sleep and sank into a dreamless doze, to be awoken next morning by activity outside the front door where our towing vehicle had been parked. The radiator water had frozen. The driver lit a fire beneath the motor to get it started. It was already past dawn. 'Get aboard!' the order rang out, and soon we set off, mummified head to toe in blankets. The problem with our field boots was that they fitted so tightly that no space was left for air to warm inside them.

Our vehicle rumbled along a log road, a kind of narrow highway to which we would become accustomed over the next couple of years. They were made by binding the trunks of pine and beech trees side by side, a very laborious job. In the swamp regions they were the only means of keeping the supply line to the front open to some extent, but they were not always successful in the periods of autumn and spring mud.

Despite the cold, which got worse in the morning hours, I kept my eyes on the road we were following. Occasionally it ran through relatively narrow forest aisles hacked in the swampy woods and on either side – more often than we liked – we saw panzers frozen into the swamp higher than half-track height. Between them now and again an 8.8-cm flak gun, each with many white rings painted around the barrel, the tally of its victims. We had not seen

A Bofors 40-mm anti-aircraft gun seen after capture by the Wehrmacht. Guns of this Swedish design were licence-built and used by many nations during World War II. In the background is Riga rail terminus.

this before. When infantrymen at a stop enquired of us if it was 'still open to our rear', we gradually became aware of the dubious situation into which we were entering.

Long beforehand we knew by the artillery fire and shells exploding not too far ahead that we were approaching the front. At a fork in the road just before Tikhvin was a Russian 52-tonner [KV-2 heavy tank] which had been destroyed in action. It was the first time we had seen a monster of this size. For one of our 3.7-cm anti-tank guns to even think of engaging a tank like that was crazy, only an 8.8-cm flak gun was equal to the task, at fairly close range, and the Russians had dozens of these steel giants. Probably we have the 88s to thank that a total catastrophe did not occur in the first winter.

We reached Tikhvin. It consisted mainly of wooden houses, but of better quality than those I described earlier. The carpentry of the interior was less rough, and the exteriors were often adorned with wood carvings. Probably no house here had escaped damage, either from shelling or fire. In the north-west of the town was a huge whitewashed religious establishment with several large onion-type turrets. The radio team went there because the regiment chose it for its command centre.

The sky was cloudless but assumed an odd pale reddish colour as a weak sun rose over the snow-covered streets of the town. We were ordered to dismount and walk the rest of the way to the monastery. At the various forks in the road, a tree of metal tactical signs would point the way to each individual command post. The town looked deserted except for the occasional Wehrmacht motorcycle or Volkswagen amphibious car passing us. 'Look lively there!' we were ordered on several occasions. Suddenly we came under salvoes of artillery fire. The Russians could see over the town and fired at everything recognised as enemy. Now we knew why we were supposed to look lively.

We were received by Leutnant Dr Hubatsch at the monastery. 'Get to safety, every five minutes we have a direct hit in the courtyard.' Hannes Seifert from Litzmannstadt had been killed on his arrival and his body now lay in the courtyard with other victims. Hannes was a quiet and introverted type who never had

Following the withdrawal of the Soviets, Latvian civilians gather at the gates of a convent to hear the new military power announce its arrangements.

much contact with others. Now he joined the enormous army of the war dead.

The Russians knew that we would have sited our command posts in the massive monastery, so they subjected it accordingly to constant nuisance and heavy-mortar fire. The monastery walls were thick, however, and one could feel safe within them. The provisions warehouse was located there, too. Heinz and I had no time to look around. After setting up our radio equipment, we followed the telephone cable along the outer monastery wall to 3rd Battalion. In the large 'hedgehog' all-round defence of Tikhvin it faced east and had its command post on a slight elevation. We

Men of 162nd Infantry Regiment ready to stand down after reaching their day's objective at Riga.

realised fairly quickly that the German force itself was surrounded, for at night the starshells fired into the sky, together with salvoes of shells and rockets, betrayed the perimeter of the circle around us. The spot where the wrecked 52-tonner stood, the Masterskaya fork in the road, was the only place beyond which the telephone connection continued, that had been the reason for the anxious question repeated frequently upon our arrival as to whether it was 'still open to our rear'.

We shared an earth bunker with our defects-search troop. The previous day an *Oberleutnant* had been killed by a tank round. Therefore, early next morning, we began repairing the damage and reinforcing the bunker ceiling. Wooden beams from the nearest house were laid on top of the ceiling and then bucket after bucket of water from the nearby spring poured over them. In the prevailing temperature of –30 °C it froze at once and provided better protection combined with the beams. Inside the bunker we had a round iron stove left there by our predecessors and firewood from the surrounding houses; here we had also found a piano which Heinz, Wolfgang and I brought into the bunker. I could tinkle a few tunes, therefore my interest in the instrument. We covered the primitive entrance of boards with a blanket and now we had done most things possible to make bunker life tolerable.

From our position we looked out over a part of the town but never saw sign of the Soviets who were present there in far more substantial numbers than ourselves. Some of them were newly arrived Siberian divisions, superbly equipped for winter, quite apart from the fact that their soldiers had been accustomed since the cradle to coping with extreme cold.

Thirty-six artillery batteries had been identified around Tikhvin, together with many mortars, and for the first time a quantity of 'salvo guns' better known as the notorious 'Stalin Organs' or *Katyushas*. The principle was similar to our smoke rockets. The firing ramps were mounted on trucks and therefore very portable. They would be fired in close vicinity to the front

The field kitchen beginning to serve up in a Riga side street.

Resting in the shade of a Riga residence.

and generally change position at once to avoid being pin-pointed by our artillery. Thirty-six or more rockets could be discharged in rapid succession. They arrived at the target tremendously fast with a wide scatter across the impact area. On two occasions, near Leningrad and at Birsen in Courland, I experienced being caught out in the open under such a hail of fire and escaped unhurt.

I think that the effect on morale was greater than the actual damage. In my opinion an artillery round was deadlier by far.

At Tikhvin we not only heard the Stalin Organs for the first time but also the German '*Stuka zu Fuss*', large-calibre rockets mostly fired singly. It was said that these rockets were filled partially with compressed air so that when they exploded within a certain radius of victims they burst their lungs. The victims were recognised by the coagulated blood around their mouths. The Russians threatened to use poison gas if the use of this weapon was not discontinued. Whether the compressed air component and the Russian poison gas threat were genuine I never found out.

The frost damage which the harsh winter inflicted on men and materials was close to catastrophic. Only with great sacrifice could the fronts be stabilised to some extent. In our sector reports of deaths due to exposure to cold became ever more frequent. The clothing issued to German troops was sufficient to face a severe central European winter, but not a Russian one. In the long run, a pair of knitted gloves, ear-muffs and a greatcoat of thick material were not enough to withstand temperatures of –30 to –35 °C in the open air, yet that was what we were required to withstand – at all costs. It was worst for the feet without fur-lined boots. Despite movements and stamping, the blood would not circulate that far down. The cold in the feet was followed by a tingling sensation until a sudden apparent warmth eliminated it, and then one would feel nothing. Frostbite began at the toes, and

if no action was taken the icing-up process continued, which would result in toes, and often enough the entire foot having to be amputated. The worst pain occurred when frozen flesh began to thaw out in a warmer environment.

At Tikhvin the frost also affected weapons and equipment. It cracked open water-cooling systems in motors, broke railway lines and froze gun oil so that weapons would not work – and the life of a soldier certainly depended on that. Machine gunners kept the breeches of their weapons warm with body heat, need being the mother of invention! The high losses due to exposure to cold, added to the battle casualties which had weakened our companies over the course of the previous month, made it seem likely that the Tikhvin front must finally collapse. This caused us grave concern.

On 6 December 1941, St Nicholas's Day in Germany, a red candle girdled with silver tinsel stood on the radio casing. I had received mail and learned from my mother that my brother Oskar was serving with an infantry company in the field outside Leningrad, the poor devil. I could only hope that Oskar would receive a none too serious wound to get him sent away from the front. That was the lesser evil based on my observations of the possibilities for an infantryman. My other brother Franz was somewhere in the southern sector, in an artillery orderly office. My mother had the task of writing three letters each week.

A park in Riga after the withdrawal of the Soviets.

On the evening of 7 December we received orders to find ourselves a hand-sledge for the retreat from Tikhvin. We thought we must be mishearing. The Wehrmacht in retreat? It was depressing news but also a relief, for we knew very well that

The Latvian National Theatre in Riga dressed in the national colours after the withdrawal of the Soviet army of occupation.

we were encircled. I acquired a sledge as I had been instructed, and in the late afternoon the Russians bombarded Tikhvin with every gun they had, apparently using phosphorus shells, for the town was still burning in the evening and this helpfully lit our route out.

When night fell we gathered at the monastery. Here a great drama occurred because the paymasters defended the provisions compound with pistols drawn. They preferred to blow it up rather than let the infantry have the contents. Did the paymasters' duty extend that far? I doubt it. Too strict adherence to regulations at the wrong time can lead to grotesque results.

Finally we crept out past the burning houses. The Russians appeared not to notice. Our mood was both tense and depressed at the same time. Here and there we passed infantrymen sitting on the *Rollbahn*, their feet wrapped in straw or rags, groaning or crying with pain. Something of a thaw had set in, which brought snowfall and a lessening of the cold so that the retreat was not so grim. We were informed that the withdrawal would take place in stages to the Volkhov River where extensive positions had been prepared for us. A large bridgehead to Luk would have to be held so as to serve as the departure point for the attack operations in 1942. We were told how much ground we were expected to cover daily and how we would get there.

Once our regiment was made the rearguard and then it was very important that we did not lose contact with those ahead. Heinz and I stood at the side of the *Rollbahn* and saw how slowly the last trucks passed us by. Heinz stared at them as if hypnotised without making a move to get aboard one. I urged him, 'Man, there's nothing better than getting away from here! What are you waiting for? Want to stay with the Russians?'

The Freedom Monument in Riga.

Bouquets of flowers adorn the pedestal of the Latvian Freedom Monument, Latvian freedom fighters stand guard following the ejection of the Soviets.

Heinz didn't reply and carried on staring at the convoy of trucks. I decided to take things into my own hands. He was supposed to be my radio-team leader, but it seemed to me that his 'qualities of leadership' had deserted him temporarily. When the next truck had to slow down, I hoisted my radio set over the flap at the rear and heaved myself up after it. Heinz had no choice but to do likewise. Now he was furious: 'Do that again and I'll put a slug into you.' Soon after he calmed down. This was our only serious difference of opinion in the two years we worked together.

On another day of the retreat we were with the last units clearing a village. It would have been about four in the afternoon, pitch dark but brightly illuminated. Pioneers were busy setting alight all the village houses with benzine. Orders from above. The enemy had to be denied any possibility of finding accommodation. The cold had increased. Old people and women holding children by the hand or in their arms stood crying before their burning houses. One woman pointed to her children and pleaded, '*Malinki, malinki!*' – 'The children, the children!' It was a waking nightmare. Surely it was not possible in real life to burn down the homes of these people in this bitter cold? This time it had not been the decision of an individual army commander, but a general order. This image of inhumanity was again one of these memories which I have found unforgettable: burning houses in a biting frost at night leaving women and children crying outside. I was a weakling, not hard like Krupp steel, for otherwise I could not have had these feelings. For any disciplined army it is so, it might even have been necessary, but where is the humanity, the compassion for those weaker than oneself, the unarmed?

Yet there was humanity. A few days later our radio troop was attached to a platoon of infantry which had to carry out security duties in the area of Luk, a little off the road of the retreat. At this time it had already become clear that for several reasons the Luk bridgehead could not be held, and in addition 215th Division, which had been brought up from France, had had its line penetrated at several places with serious losses. Its orders today were to hold a small village until a certain hour and then pull out after burning down all the houses. Heinz and I were sitting with the platoon leader, an *Unteroffizier* and some of his men, in a clean house inhabited by an old married couple and a middle-aged woman with two children. They received us in a friendly manner, the samovar hummed on the table, outside the sun shone down on a glittering winter landscape. Everything was quiet and peaceful. The women offered us tea served in porcelain cups. We accepted and thanked them for it. The hour came to move out, and we picked up our weapons and equipment. 'So now I'm supposed to set fire to their house. Well I don't think so,' the

Unteroffizier muttered more to himself than to us. 'March off!' None of his soldiers spoke up to remind him of the orders.

In the late evening we found ourselves somewhere in a forest glade by one of those camp fires which blazed up everywhere during that retreat. Our bodies were roasted at the front, our backs remained deeply frozen. In the centre of the body there was a mixture of heat and cold. It was difficult in those days to keep cheerful.

Later I forced my way into a totally crammed and overheated house of two floors and inveigled myself between the infantry lying together like sardines in a tin in the hope of getting a few hours' sleep in the warm. But sleep was not possible. Itching and scratching advertised the presence of lice, something new again! The things we had to put up with! They would plague us over all the years we spent in Russia, sometimes reinforced by various other kinds of bug.

CHAPTER 6

On the Volkhov Front

WE CROSSED THE VOLKHOV RIVER towards evening on 23 December 1941. The weather had taken a turn for the better and now it snowed. The wind had dropped and one could hear the snowflakes falling. We plodded easily through the fresh snow and reached the village of Dmitrovka near Chudovo. The regimental command post was to remain there for several months.

Almost at the same time as our infantry companies arrived, Russian reconnaissance troops reached the banks of the frozen-over Volkhov. The burning down of the village houses had therefore not held up the Siberians. The worst thing was that the promised 'previously prepared positions' did not exist – perhaps in other sectors but not in ours.

The retreat ended. It was certainly exemplary, well-ordered and carried out, bringing back all transportable equipment and weapons in the most abysmal weather conditions by a division which had been on active service every day since 22 June and, lacking all necessary clothing and preparation, had had to hold out against newly arrived, superbly clothed enemy forces. Most of the panzers and artillery bogged down in the swamps had to be destroyed by limpet mines. In a bulletin our army corps described it as a glorious page in German military history, but what good did that do? Fur boots would have been better. What Hitler said in his speech in January 1942 marking the ninth anniversary of his seizure of power was more to the point when he called the achievements of the German soldier in this winter battle 'a heroic epic'. All those who took part in it know that on this occasion he was not exaggerating.

A rest by the wayside, Latvia, summer 1941.

On Christmas night, we of the regimental signals platoon sat together fairly complete in numbers in a Russian wooden house. That afternoon a fir tree had been cut down at the southern edge of Dmitrovka village and set up in a room adorned with strips of tinsel and candles. Though not much more than a sapling, in the warm room it exuded a pleasant aroma reminiscent of the

Harz. The candles were lit and Leutnant Dr Hubatsch had us gather round the tree while he read to us the poem '*Kriegsweihnacht*' – 'War Christmas' – by Walter Flex, a soldier of the Great War. As a historian, Leutnant Hubatsch very often found parallels between past and present.

As soon as the festivities terminated, Heinz and I were sent without radio equipment to 2nd Battalion at Pertetshno, two or three kilometres from the new front. As we stepped out into the dark night and followed the messenger who led us to the battalion, we could hear the carol '*Hohe Nacht der klaren Sterne*' – 'Holy Night of Clear Stars' – being sung behind us. The night was not clear, and a light snow flurry whipped our faces. We drew our heads in . . .

We arrived just in time for the Christmas roast chicken, bottles of frozen wine which we literally had to crack open, and frozen bread, chopped with a hatchet or cut with a bayonet. At least we had a roof over our heads while our comrades of the infantry companies had to stand watch in the open or work frenetically building bunkers. The frozen earth required hand grenades and explosives to loosen it, then trench digging would proceed without delay. It was high time too, for the Russians had now closed up along a broad front on the other bank of the Volkhov. Immediately after Christmas the battalion staff left the village and dug in at the edge of the wood on the plain by the railway embankment.

Once we signals people had loosened the ground we set to in three groups. Entrenching tools, hatchets, saws and nails were made available. One group cut down some pine trees, the second sawed them into the necessary lengths and the third transported all of these to the embryonic bunker, already excavated to a depth of 170 centimetres. Four sturdy tree trunks went into the ground as support columns, wired up to prevent their falling inwards, and two layers of thick tree stems served as the ceiling. The whole thing was covered over with the earth spoil and now the bunker was almost ready, only the sanitary section had to be created. An empty fuel barrel was converted into a stove and an appropriate place hewn for it. A stove pipe was added, but where it came from I have no idea.

We moved in after two days. The heating worked – the tree trunks sweated so much that water trickled down the 'walls'. We had a place capable of being heated for our stay in the woods, and had some certainty we would not receive a direct hit, or at least not while trees stood around us to intercept the flight of incoming shells. If the Russians fired delayed action munitions that was another matter of course.

We were already dug-in when the Russian artillery completed moving up and began calibrating its field of fire. The ranging rounds and little clouds of smoke reached beyond Dmitrovka and Pertetshno. Our advanced telephone exchange at Pertetshno received a direct hit but this only interrupted telephone communications for a short while. The two telephonists escaped with a fright.

At the end of December the fierce cold returned, temperatures of −30 °C and more. On New Year's Eve Heinz and I celebrated with the men of 2nd Battalion signals. We had schnapps and I took a flash photo of the event with powder from two bullets. Later I sent the historic picture to my female pen-friend in Memel, and she took it with her when the time came to flee, and so at least I have some photos from this time.

New Year's Eve was not yet ended for I had one hour's sentry duty outside our bunker as from 2300 hrs. Sentries were lent a pair

An assault party of 162nd Infantry Regiment proudly presenting a number of captured Russian weapons in July 1941. In the foreground is a Russian Maxim machine-gun on a wheeled chassis, along with a light MG, a light mortar, rifles and other items.

An *Oberfeldwebel* of the assault party demonstrates how the Maxim machine-gun was handled.

A horse-drawn supply waggon crossing a river in the Baltic region, July 1941.

Above & right: Russian prisoners taken by men of 61st Infantry Division.

of large fur over-boots. Despite that I froze terribly, particularly my feet. One had to be constantly active, swinging the arms for warmth, moving the feet, rubbing the nose. The snow squeaked so much under my steps that it set my teeth on edge. Something cracked in the woods. Russians? Should I raise the alarm? No, the weight of ice now on the trees from the hoar frost had grown heavier causing a branch or two to snap. The glow of starshell fired at the front could be seen between the treetops; from Volkhov one heard short bursts of machine-gun fire and single rounds from rifles. Nearby all was quiet, only the crunch of one's own steps and frozen breath. Subconsciously I perceived an initially soft incoming noise and then mortar bombs landed less than thirty metres from me. The night fell quiet again except for the racket at the front. Now and again stray explosive rounds struck the branches of trees, red flares soared up and scattered in all directions before burning out.

The moon had risen, the blanket of snow on the plain beyond the edge of the woods shone brightly between the trees. Heinz arrived punctually at midnight to relieve me. We exchanged mutual good wishes for the coming year just before our companies' pyrotechnic display began, greeting the New Year in their own way with flares in all available colours, long bursts of machine-gun fire and shooting from hand-held weapons. The Russians

must have been surprised that we had such a surplus of munitions to waste. I was too frozen to care, disappeared into the bunker, took a swig from my flask, put some wood in the stove fire, crept under the blankets and fell asleep.

I was awoken early next morning by an excited but restrained voice. 'Alarm! Alarm! Put the fire out! Everybody out of the bunker! Tanks!'

'Don't be daft, New Year is over!'

'*Russian* tanks!' Unteroffizier Grau shouted and was already outside with his carbine. Now one could hear quite clearly the approaching growl of the heavy motors. Sheltering behind thick tree trunks we beheld three tanks rumbling along the path scarcely thirty metres from the edge of the wood, heading for 3rd Battalion command post near the railway embankment. There was even a bold Russian tank commander standing up in the turret hatch. Then they stopped; I assumed they did not dare go any farther without infantry . . .

The man in the hatch suddenly collapsed and was hauled below. One of us had shot him. The hatch cover was pulled shut. Rudi Sänger, a telegraphist with 3rd Battalion signals staff climbed aboard one of the tanks and hammered with his fists on the hatch cover. Helpless rage was useless against a steel colossus. The three tanks set off again, turned their turrets towards us and soon we heard the familiar dry report of their cannon and their hits. Two light infantry guns of 13th Company had their position directly in front of our bunker on the edge of the wood. A wheel from a gun flew off. The tanks'

A Russian T-26 tank destroyed by 162nd Infantry Regiment, summer 1941.

machine guns chattered and fire rippled the length of the woods. I threw myself down in the snow. The tanks held to the field paths and returned to their lines, crossing the frozen Volkhov River.

On 3 January I had just fetched replacement batteries from regiment and was returning to 2nd Battalion when a tremendous artillery barrage began, and an endless series of explosions raged

Covered in dust , men of 162nd Infantry Regiment rest by the wayside, summer 1941. Recognisable by his Red Cross armband (extreme right) is a *Sanitäter* (medic).

along the entire front. It was clear that this must be the prelude to a major Russian offensive. The brunt of the fire was borne by our infantry positions and what I assumed were our artillery emplacements. I hurried to the battalion, giving a wide berth to a 10.5-cm battery at the edge of Pertetshno woods. As I reached the command post night was falling, which occurred at about 1430 hrs in December and January, earlier in certain weather conditions.

Following the softening-up by their artillery, the Russians attacked along the whole front, but our companies had a good field of fire over the Volkhov and the barrier fire of our own artillery warded off their attack. To the south of us they had broken through the neighbouring front line and by night they appeared behind our command post making their ugly cries of '*Urra!*' Dressed in white camouflage suits and snow shoes, these Siberians – mostly Mongols – swept through our thin screening line cutting down everybody in their path. Apparently their design was to roll up our front from the flank and later from the rear, when strong forces appeared behind the lines of our neighbour on the right, the 162nd, holding the small Grusino bridgehead. After the second breakthrough that night it was clear to the battalion staff that we were cut off. The crank starter on field telephone 33 was slack: the telephone repairs staff could not be sent out by night across enemy-held territory and we set up the Morse transceiver. By means of encoded Morse messages,

Men of 162nd Infantry Regiment move into positions for an attack on an airfield in Estonia. An observer (right, above) assesses the situation.

regiment announced that the situation would be rectified the following morning. As good as their word, at 1000 hrs two self-propelled assault guns came up with a battalion from 161st

Regiment, 81st Infantry Division, to force the supply routes open. Once the Russians had been driven out, our troops occupied the supply road between our command post and Pertetshno – in temperatures of –30 °C, no shelter, simply lying in the snow! They had no field of fire, for just beyond the roadway, eight to ten metres wide, was fairly impenetrable undergrowth, deeply snowed under. At any moment Russian ski troops could appear from there.

In this bitter cold, the men of 161st Regiment had pitched their tents and shovelled snow over them to help keep in the warmth. They were as poorly clad for the winter as we were. The pitiful sight was soon concealed by the early nightfall. Scarcely had our companies been supplied with provisions and ammunition than more ugly cries of '*Urra!*' resounded through the darkness. Then came the swish of countless skiers, gliding in fast; a few minutes' shooting, metallic noises, commands rasped from hoarse, rough throats, the cries of the dying – silence. The Russians were through again. Our soldiers only saw, or anticipated too late, the swift arrival of well-camouflaged expert ski troops without warning at the shortest range, and were literally overwhelmed and butchered.

All telephone connections to the rear were interrupted again as they had been the previous day: the following day the supply tracks were re-opened. Our losses were far greater than those of the Russians. Almost all the fallen were Germans. Wolfgang von Ulardt and Willi Gerk, who had long since given away his horses and reverted to being a telephonist, followed the attacking German troops in order to restore the telephone connections. The Russians had cut away hundreds of metres of cable which now had to be replaced. Suddenly Willi threw up his arms and fell backwards, shot through the heart. His premonition at Quimper had been fulfilled. A single round had ended his life, fired by a Russian sniper from concealment. The Russians had many of them.

A few days later when combing the woods between the forest paths and the plain we found the lengths of cable. The Russians had used it to bind their German prisoners to trees, and after breaking

An *Unteroffizier* buttons a fallen comrade into a burial cape.

their wrists had left them to die of cold. There were some Sudeten Germans amongst the victims as one could tell from identity tabs sewn to their greatcoats. What I have described above occurred on two or more occasions. Then it fell relatively quiet, the weight of the Russian attacks shifting to the area of 215th Infantry Division south of us.

Next the Russians pushed forward in large groups behind our lines and rattled the various rearward services. They were cut off, however, and had to make their way back across the Volkhov to their own lines. It was probably 10 January 1942 when our neighbouring regiment warned of Russian movements behind our main front towards 2nd and 3rd Battalions. The 3rd Battalion command post lay at the far end of the plain by a railway embankment. Messengers, signals people and the 13th Company gun crews had to take up positions for self-defence at the edge of the woods. Only the telephone exchange remained manned. One heavy and one light machine gun were withdrawn from the front and brought to our position for support. Actually it was the other way round, we supported the machine guns.

The sky was overcast and the night pitch dark, only the occasional flare at the front or over the plain provided temporary illumination. It was still bitterly cold. Finally the report came that the Russian force had just passed the 3rd Battalion command post and was moving across the plain. A breathless silence held sway as we stared unseeing into the darkness. 'There, there they are. Don't shoot, let them get closer,' was whispered down the line. In the centre of the plain a grey shadow appeared, several metres broad. It might have been a bush, I couldn't make out any movement. I had still not seen any Russians, not even when machine guns and mortars, also present to support us, opened fire, together with all our carbines. The whole thing was over in less than five minutes.

Now the battlefield was lit by starshell. About fifty dead Russians lay spread around, not far from the woods. A seriously wounded commissar or officer still had the strength to raise his head and his pistol and shoot a hated 'Fascist' through the chest before receiving a hail of fire himself. His round hit the sergeant of the machine-gun platoon and wounded him severely.

Weeks later the fallen Russians still lay where they had fallen in the frozen snow of the plain, all unshod. Fur boots were the most coveted item of apparel for Wehrmacht soldiers in the Russian winter of 1941. They were removed immediately from dead Russians before they froze stiff. The valuable boots of the Russian fallen substituted for what the Wehrmacht had not thought to make available for its own troops.

After having been a senior commander in the defence of Moscow, on 7 January 1942 Lieutenant General Andrey Andreyevich Vlasov, commander of the Soviet 2nd Army, initiated an attempt to lift the siege of Leningrad. Three armies on which he was relying failed to advance in time. Nevertheless, by February 1942,

Vlasov's assault army had crossed the Volkhov and advanced seventy-five kilometres between the German lines on the west side of the river. Soon, however, Vlasov's force found itself cut off and unable to receive reinforcements and ammunition. The swamps thawed in April 1942 by when Vlasov had still received no help by air or land and Stalin refused him permission to retreat. His army ate its horses during the encirclement. On 14 May 1942 the Germans attacked and only then did Vlasov receive the order to make for the other bank of the river. By then he had been declared a traitor to the Soviet Union and had lost the greater part of his army. Consequently he had no alternative but to lead the survivors through woods and swamps towards the Germans, to whom he surrendered at Silverskaya on 6 July.

1st Battalion returned in late June or early July. That was how long the Volkhov encirclement lasted, and ended with the wiping out of the bulk of General Vlasov's troops. The fighting was hard and bitter. The encircled Russians resorted to cannibalism in some cases. I took no part in these battles. Signals staff leader Oberfeldwebel Schilwa laughed ironically and told me, 'We always thought it couldn't get any worse! I just don't believe that any longer.'

CHAPTER 7

Spring and Summer 1942: On the Volkhov

WHAT WE HAD NOT THOUGHT POSSIBLE after the events of the first days in January came to pass. Our sector on the Volkhov front fell silent – and this for quite a while. Apart from scouting parties and assault troop activity there was nothing else exciting to write home about. The small Russian bridgehead, the so-called *Kastenwald*, was flattened in the late spring by two of our heavy infantry guns which we called 'Jumbo'. The effect of their 15-cm shells must have been devastating.

Then there was quiet. That does not mean that we could sit back and relax, for the men of the infantry companies continued being constantly involved in trench building and other digging work. They had very little time for sleep. The company strengths had been much reduced by losses and these were replaced so sparingly that barely half the wartime authorised strength was being maintained. At best this meant five or six men to do the work where there should have been nine. As a result they could not have more than a couple of hours' sleep per night, and what they got was continually disturbed by the lice infestation.

Heinz Schimanski and I were transferred to 2nd Battalion in the railway embankment. In the reorganisation, the regiment had been reduced to two battalions, making a virtue out of necessity. Therefore the effective 'trench strength' of a regiment was now only a third of what it had been when the Russian campaign started.[1] I would only have mentioned this out of interest should I not have been affected by it personally.

Soldiers of 162nd Infantry Regiment taking leave of their fallen comrades-in-arms.

Our bunkers had been created by excavating into the side of the three-metre high railway embankment. Above our bunker, in the centre of the disused permanent way, now stood a 5-cm and

a 7.5-cm anti-tank gun. The Wehrmacht had learned its lesson and after the bad experiences of the past year had acted promptly.

For Heinz and me, the main activity was fighting the plague of lice and obtaining firewood. The latter was no problem for in the woods to the right of the embankment grew several kinds of birch tree whose wood burned even when wet. Birch-bark replaced paper. Though the hovel filled with acrid fumes when the wood was lit, it did not take long before we had a warming fire in the round iron stove. Snow boiled in a mess tin and kept refilled provided wonderfully soft water for tea. The supplies of provisions kept coming and the midday meal from the battalion kitchen was always better than that at regimental HQ. This was the achievement of the cook. Therefore we would have been content had it not been for the lice.

Lice are those tiny crawling insects which cannot hop or fly and live on blood, which means digging into your skin to find the source. The continual scratching resulted in scabs. With increasing warmth they became especially active. My fine brown woollen pullover was one of their favourite haunts; particularly around the collar one found their nits and lice of all ages. We thought that if they liked the warm, perhaps the cold would kill them and so we experimented. One cold February night with thirty degrees of frost, we laid out our pullovers on the bunker roof all night, and next morning found the lice all seemingly dead, covered with hoar frost; but no sooner was warmth applied than they recovered with an appetite and were more aggressive. So, until a remedy was found much later, we had to put up with them.

It was dangerous to leave the bunker in the evening, not only on account of the cold but also for the indirect fire of Russian machine guns. When dusk fell the gunners occupied their foremost positions and began shooting, and so one did not stay outside the bunker without good cause. The used explosive rounds with red tracer to keep the railway embankment under fire while at the same time the '*UvD*' (*Unteroffizier vom Dienst* – 'Duty Corporal') would make his appearance. These aircraft, which we nicknamed 'sewing machines' for the noise of their motor, were slow biplanes which concentrated mainly on harassing the *Tross* by dropping a single bomb in each attack. Early on they dropped artillery shells fitted with a stabiliser. We didn't take them seriously, although they were a nuisance and once when they hit our divisional bakery and set it afire we had to eat crispbread for a whole week. Crispbread was not filling and required a lot of chewing, and so most men considered it inedible. The *UvD* maintained the nuisance raids and the buzzing of its motor soon became part of life by the River Volkhov.

In this epoch of reconnaissance activity, mention must be made of a name well-known in the regiment, Feldwebel Listat from Tilsit. On many occasions he crossed the frozen Volkhov with his patrol, crept through the Russian lines and reconnoitred kilometres-deep into the enemy hinterland. His observations raised eyebrows in high quarters, as for example when he discovered that in the Russian rear area there was almost no military presence but yet their supply system functioned well. We asked ourselves how that was possible, for the German side required more military in the rear areas than at the front, but we knew that the Russian system worked, for they never seemed to lack ammunition.

One day the *Feldwebel* and his party failed to return. They had already been listed as missing when he reported back with

Fallen soldiers of 162nd Infantry Regiment laid out prior to burial.

Clearly moved, Hauptmann Gottfried Weber enters a grave to take leave of his fallen soldiers.

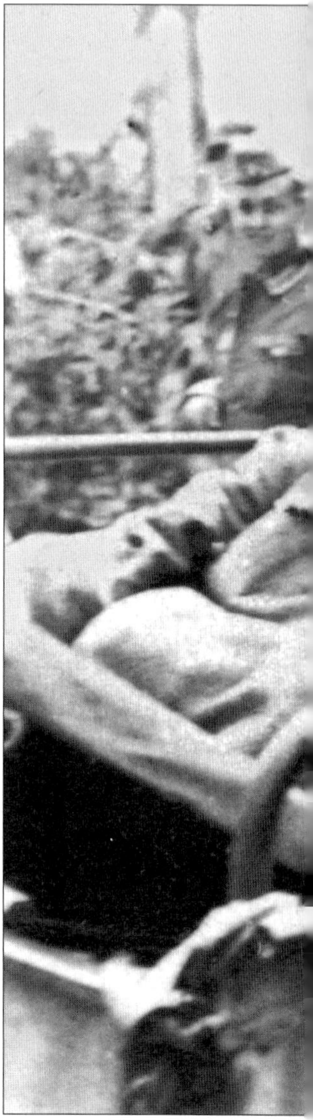

his patrol three days later. His compass had frozen and he had lost his bearings. This dare-devil soldier and wearer of the German Cross in Gold lost his life in the summer of 1942 in the following way. He was angling on the banks of the Volkhov between our minefields whose position he knew exactly. It must have been some fish to make him forget the danger, for in his struggle to land it he trod on one of our mines.

Towards the end of February 1942 I received a letter from my mother informing me that my elder brother Oskar had fallen near Leningrad on 12 December. His grave was at the church of Krasny Bor. In her letter she wrote: 'His industrious hands rest for ever. I simply cannot believe it. I would like to disinter him with my bare hands and stroke his black locks. But I must not show my grief. I must be the stronger one. Father cries. He reproaches himself that he had him for too short a time. He sighs and groans for his son every night.' I could not bear to read any more of it, I cried too and was not ashamed to do so. Heinz noticed. He did not enquire or make any attempt to console me but said nothing and expressed his sympathy in the best way.

In the early months of 1942, the 'sewing machines' dropped tons of leaflets for us to read. Typical snippets which I recall are: 'Come over to us! We are workers and farmers like most of yourselves. Why shoot at us?' And: 'Take leave until the end of the war. Thousands of beautiful women here are waiting for you. You will be given soup three times per day,

Russian female prisoners in military greatcoats brought in by 162nd Infantry Regiment.

jam and chocolate pudding!' We used to sneer at these offers, but sometimes the leaflets made one or other infantryman reflect. For example, at the time in 1943 when the Italians left the Axis and many of them arrived in Germany as prisoners: 'You are here, and risking your life on foreign soil. And at the same time the Italians are bedding your wives and daughters. Simply go home, or come over to us.' However, considering our own experience of the Russians, I do not believe that this propaganda made a single German soldier waver.

Sometimes now we found things to laugh at. A soldier of the infantry company received a letter from his previous billet in East Prussia. His contact with a girl there had apparently not been without its consequences for she had written making the most drastic threats. It gave the whole company something to laugh about, if not the recipient of the letter.

In March 1942, Heinz and I moved into a larger bunker where we joined the telephone linesmen, Wolfgang, and Fritz Krebs and some men from the signals staff of 2nd Battalion. The battalion telephone exchange was also located here and very soon we had set up the battalion commander's radio, plugged in earphones and fitted them to the lid of a mess tin. The loudspeaker was now ready and could listen in to the music broadcast by the Soldatensender station.[2] It provided a refuge into a dreamworld to enable us to remain steady mentally.

The time came when the sun rose higher and the days grew longer. The thaw arrived and so did the winter woollies from home. In April! The Volkhov was in flood and burst its banks. Day and night the mines laid in the winter exploded. The river banks and the plain were swamped, but the waters did not reach us in the railway embankment. Some of the front-line bunkers had to be evacuated, their occupants taking to the trees. There was an almost total lull in the fighting, both sides had enough to do coping with the water. Footbridges were made from tree to tree, rubber boots were issued; the frozen swamps thawed and turned to mud.

Wolfgang and Fritz were constantly in the field attending to short-circuits in the telephone wiring. Especially at patches and splits in the cable the water would soak into the fibres. The crank handle of field telephone 33 was difficult to turn. When the terrain caused problems, the wiring was strung from tree to tree.

The period of mud affected the *Tross* and supply units immensely, not so much in our Chudovo sector but much more so in the areas north and south of us. Here the poor horses had to wade through mud often a metre deep pulling heavy waggons loaded with provisions and ammunition. They looked as haggard as old nags from the drudgery and torment and frequently gave up, dropped and died. Their carcasses were to be found all along the supply routes. The drivers of these horse-drawn waggons did not have it easy either and often looked as if they had been wallowing in the mud. Despite the many log roads, it was difficult to keep the troops supplied in such times but it was done.

May came. Birch, poplar and alders enlivened the swampy scenery with their delicate green. Sometimes the evenings were warm. We enjoyed exposing our naked upper bodies to the sun to heal the lice scabs. The battalion commander put weir baskets in the nearby brooks. Lampreys were a speciality here. The baskets were sometimes found empty having been raided by passing soldiers. An almost fully grown elk calf which unfortunately strayed into the field of fire of one of our machine guns was roasted in fillets but remained fairly tough.

When the enemy situation permitted, in these spring days almost overnight the bunkers acquired hedges and garden benches of white birch. Everybody took the trouble to make his 'home' as comfortable as possible. Security against direct hits played a secondary role but soon such joys were marred by a new plague, countless thousands of mosquitoes. They were particularly worrisome if any part of the body were exposed. They could be deterred by smoke but in any case we were issued face veils and at night nailed jute sacking around our beds, checking it carefully for any gaps and keeping a listening watch for the fine hum if one slipped through.

The crews of a Panzer IV and a light armoured reconnaissance car meet with men of 162nd Infantry Regiment.

Burial ceremony for fallen soldiers of 162nd Infantry Regiment brought by lorry from the field hospital to the cemetery.

In this latitude at this time of year there was no true night in mid-summer, only a two-hour period after 2300 hrs when twilight merged with grey dawn. The atmosphere this created is difficult to describe. Some men suffered from a kind of 'bunker neurosis' caused by being cooped up for weeks without any special activity to keep us occupied. Having our freedom of movement limited by water and mud and the monotony of the bunker left many desolate, inclined to irritation, aggression and playing the fool, often dangerously. For example, one evening the bunker community was sitting together unsuspectingly. Suddenly a deafening whistle resounded from the lit stove. Everybody threw themselves to the floor in the expectation of an explosion of some kind. Nothing happened. For fun, somebody outside had dropped a whistling pyrotechnic signal cartridge into the stove pipe. On another occasion a company commander returning from a patrol of inspection fired a salvo from his machine-pistol into the stove pipe of one of his companies' bunkers and thought it great fun to see all the bunker occupants come tumbling out in fright. These are two examples of abnormal behaviour which may be classified as 'bunker neurosis'.

The anti-tank company of the regiment had a ventriloquist, Oberschütze Gustl Ickler from Swabia. He had been demoted several times for playing the fool but always managed to regain his rank again quite easily. One evening he decided to visit our bunker, where a round of skat was being played. He sat to one

The battle for Estonia in the late summer of 1941 cost many lives for 61st Infantry Division

Graves marked by rough crosses.

side watching. Suddenly – quite some distance away but just perceptible – we heard 'Help! Help!' The game went on, then the cry came again, much clearer this time. Carbines were picked up and the skat players went outside to listen. Only Ickler remained in the bunker. 'Come back inside,' he said, 'It was me.' Then he demonstrated his talent, how he threw his voice without moving his mouth. Some distance away they now heard clearly, 'You

bread-heads!' Everybody laughed and went back to the skat table. Gustl had had his fun, and so had we.

During the era of the bunker neurosis, Heinz Schimanski had his own hobby to keep him quiet. He would sit in the tailor's chair, the lid of the radio field pack on his knees as a support and by candlelight he was lost in himself sketching and painting French women on postcards. Blondes, brunettes and always with the sensuous longing look in their eyes, nude of course. This fantasy of a deprived man was inexhaustible, conjuring up each mirage like a man dying of thirst in the desert. Oberfeldwebel Reuter came in complaining, 'This is dreadful. Wherever you go you find Schimanski's sissies.' Heinz looked up with an embarrassed ironic smile, inhaled deeply on his cigarette and kept painting. Wolfgang looked over his shoulder and said, 'Heinz, you're a dirty old man.'

We were bored. Then the idea came to me to find myself a female pen-friend. Thinking it over I remembered the telephone trunk-call exchange at Tilsit when we were in East Prussia. At Gut Kleinscharlack during the routine evening tests that the line was still intact we would often exchange banter with the female switchboard operators. We had the impression that they were nice girls, and in any case Tilsit had the reputation of having many pretty girls. 'Heinz, we should write to the Tilsit trunk-call exchange.' I explained my motive, he agreed, and so we each wrote a letter to an unknown girl there. We put the two letters in a single envelope and wrote our names on the back:

A long row of graves bordering the road of advance.

'Obergefreiter Heinz Schimanski and Gefreiter Erhard Steiniger, field post number 04041' and mailed it.

I went off on leave at the end of May 1942, the first since I had been called up in October 1940! My mother had made enquiries at the Army office because inheritance matters had to be worked out following the death of my elder brother. Ahead of the locomotive of the leave train were coupled two flat waggons for anti-mine protection, especially necessary in the partisan area around Luga, and a 2-cm flak gun was positioned at the centre of the train. My father offered me the farm as my brother's heir. He knew I wanted to remain in my profession as a cereals trader. It never worked out, however; in 1945 the Sudeten Germans were liberated again, but this time deprived of homeland and property.

When I returned to Volkhov, two letters from girls at the Tilsit phone exchange were waiting for me. Heinz had also received one. I could hardly write to both of mine and so I made my choice based on the handwriting. I let Wolfgang have the other letter. So from now on began for me the correspondence with the unknown *Fräulein* which was to last all my life. As I write this I can hear her busy in the kitchen preparing the East Prussian recipe Christmas marzipan which our grandchildren love so much.

Fine weather in this latitude dried out the swamps and made them passable, as the deep frost had done in winter. Hostilities recommenced. Our two bridgeheads on the Volkhov were a thorn in the flesh of the Russians who began a series of long-lasting concentrated attacks. Our neighbouring 162nd Regiment had to fight bravely to hold the small Grusino bridgehead: the larger Kirishi bridgehead was in the 21st East Prussian Division sector with whose signals reserve company I had begun my glorious military career. The heaviest fighting raged over those weeks at the two bridgeheads. We could discern this from the distant artillery barrages.

On the other hand an illegal private 'armistice' had been agreed between our company (the 7th under Oberleutnant Krüger) and a Russian infantry company: for three days there was no shooting and the soldiers sunbathed at their positions. The 'armistice' was the major talking point up to divisional level. Russians and Germans waved to each other with bottles of schnapps and invited the other side to visit: both sides baulked at doing so – the trust could not extend that far. Two hours before it was scheduled to end the Russians suddenly opened fire on us. Either their company had been relieved or the two-hour time difference between Moscow and Berlin was the reason for the 'breach'.

As mentioned, the swamplands had dried up to a certain extent by August and the Russians embarked on an offensive from Leningrad, its aim being to break the encirclement in order to

A grave for six fallen comrades being dug at the wayside following an action.

guarantee supply to the city overland. In the winter, Leningrad had needed to be supplied across the ice of Lake Ladoga. Besides a 'road' for trucks, a railway had been laid down across the lake. It was attacked and broken almost every day by the Luftwaffe but nevertheless supplies still managed to get through. At a measured distance in snowdrifts on both sides of the railway skilfully camouflaged rail depots had been set up and igloos built for the railway maintenance gangs who were busy around the clock. Each group had a prescribed section of track for which it was responsible. Army High Command was surprised that, despite intense aerial attacks, the supplies were rolling again after a few hours.

For the Russians it was an absolute necessity to establish the overland route now. All the fighting between Lake Ladoga and Leningrad was concentrated on the great railway junction at Mga, beginning regularly in the first ten days of January, in summer from mid-August. The first great Russian offensive to liberate Leningrad began in August 1942. The attack was not unexpected. At this time our regiment was in army reserve – but only for a few days before being pitched into the fray in battalions under the leadership of other headquarters. Our regimental staff followed

after a march of several days to the vicinity of the new operational area.

On the way towards Nevabogen-Leningrad we passed many well-cared for cemeteries. One day the monotony of our progress was interrupted suddenly by quickly increasing aircraft noise. A Russian biplane roared overhead at barely eighty metres altitude firing at us: a Messerschmitt Bf 109 was close behind it spraying the enemy aircraft with cannon fire. Shaken, we watched as the Russian pilot abandoned his burning aircraft, which plunged into the woods 150 metres ahead of us. It all happened in a matter of seconds. We were thrilled by the aerial victory. The Russian pilot was found hanging dead in the trees.

Whilst our infantry company at Nevabogen was losing men in close combat and counter-attacks, we of the regimental signals platoon were given quarters at Shablino. This settlement was nothing like the previous Russian villages of our experience. Although consisting almost exclusively of wooden houses, one could distinctly feel here the influence of Leningrad. They were single-storey structures with carvings on the façades and insides. At even the humblest house flowers and vegetables were cultivated in the gardens. I had my hair cut at the barber's shop in Shablino and learned that Krasny Bor was only sixteen kilometres farther on towards Leningrad. I resolved to visit my brother's grave and Feldwebel Hofer, who had taken over the platoon from Leutnant Hubatsch, granted me one day's leave.

Wrapped in blankets or capes, the six fallen share a common grave.
It was in fact a disciplinary offence to take such photos.

Carrying a bouquet of flowers which a Russian girl cut from her garden with much sympathy, I went to the Leningrad *Rollbahn*, an asphalt road which connected Leningrad with

Moscow. I hitched a lift; at this time the advance of our 'Army of the Crimea' which, after the conquest of Sebastopol was intending to capture Leningrad next, was heading north but the Russians had anticipated it. The wooded areas left and right of the *Rollbahn* were crammed with our gun batteries and an absolute ban on shooting was in force in order not to betray their presence to the enemy. Somehow the Russians had got wind of it, however, and attempted to disrupt it by bombing. A few kilometres before Krasny Bor, fighter-bombers roared over, bombing the woods and *Rollbahn*. The driver and I took cover in a roadside ditch: his truck was not damaged and we suffered no harm. Finally we reached Krasny Bor.

Its wooden church stood beside the *Rollbahn*, surrounded by a small local cemetery which also had several rows of graves of German fallen. Occasionally the cemetery came under artillery fire, as could be seen by the shell craters between the graves, and the damage to the church tower. Understandably all the graves were overgrown with weeds. I had to push these aside to read what was written on the crosses. In the second row to the right facing the entrance to the church I found my brother's grave. The marker was a simple cross made from a wooden crate, the crossbeam bore his name and details, the horizontal stake was damaged by a shell splinter. I pulled up the weeds, filled the broad-necked vase I had brought with water from the cemetery spring, half dug-in the vase and placed the flowers inside it. As I then stood at the graveside in reflection, my thoughts wandered to my parents. Oskar had hoped he might win the Iron Cross, he had told me once, after the first soldiers came home on leave with decorations from the Polish and French campaigns. I took two handfuls of earth from the grave, and later sent it in a cardboard carton to my mother. She had a glass shrine made, surmounted by Oskar's photograph, and placed the memorial as the centre-piece of her writing table. Later she placed my own Iron Cross Second Class with it.

During my absence at Shablino the battalion commander, Major Rooch, and his adjutant, Oberleutnant Wippern, had been killed when a shell exploded against a tree while they were being shown the position they were to take over. Oberleutnant Saint-Paul, one of the surviving original company commanders from the first days of 61st Infantry Division had also fallen and both our companies were practically wiped out. It needed only one truck to bring back the survivors, basically just the *Tross* and part of the staff. Each battalion now had a trench strength of scarcely fifty men. Hegele of the 2nd Battalion signals staff had bayoneted a Russian in the chest and seen the hate in his eyes as he died, and he had immobilised another Russian by striking the side of his face with the sharp edge of his entrenching tool. In a similar situation I would never have come out on top.

Bad though the losses seemed then, in the longer term the situation was mitigated when, after a few weeks, the walking wounded who had recuperated began to flow back, swelling the companies somewhat. Companies with fifty to eighty men were the rule while the trench strength of a wartime company was meant to be 150 men. Our regiment was now sent to a quiet sector of the front near the so-called Tigoda position in an extensive area of swamp which rarely had enough exposed sand for digging in. The regimental command post was therefore in blockhouses and Finnish tents. For entertainment we tapped the regimental commander's radio set again. The time at Tigoda was tolerable and I would have glossed over it had it not been for two events involving two of our comrades in their personal lives.

Werner Zutraun had gone to the War Academy in Berlin as an officer-aspirant. Obergefreiter Ernst Skambraks had been promoted to *Unteroffizier* to replace Unteroffizier Paukstadt, and our new regimental commander was Oberstleutnant Sperling. It was the end of 1942 and I had just returned from my second home leave. The frozen swamp had a light covering of snow, the low temperatures were tolerable. This time the winter found us

A common grave for three fallen soldiers, each mound marked by as cross, steel helmet and a wreath.

equipped. Every man had a wadded battledress, white one side and with a camouflage pattern on the other, fur boots with leather soles, fur caps and fur-lined gloves.

Card games of skat and '17 and 4' were in progress. What else was there to spend one's money on? A telephone call from the regimental commander came requesting that the field telephone be extended to his bedside for the night. Ernst Skambraks went to the commander's tent – nobody there. On the table stood a bottle of French three-star cognac. It revived in him joyful memories of Quimper and the need for a tiny swig from the bottle, to bring back those French-cognac memories – with just a drop on the tongue – proved irresistible. He moved aside the telephone, and instead of the tiny swig he had intended to have, took a big one. It left a warm feeling trickling down to his toes. His delicate palate was enraptured. Thus reinforced he steered his footsteps to the home blockhouse. Just as he was in the act of regaling his listeners ('Three stars, slid down like oil') the telephone rang. Far from the earpiece we could hear the commander's every word. 'Who repositioned the telephone here? Report yourself to me immediately with belt buckled and wearing steel helmet!'

The tragedy now ran its course. Ernst was transferred to an infantry company with immediate effect. His world fell apart and, as if sentenced to death, he packed his belongings. He bemoaned his fate: 'Yesterday the commander's darling, today ruined.' From this moment on Ernst disappeared from sight. Alcohol seldom does anybody any good, therefore when I pour myself a drop of Hennessey it is only to remember the taste of cognac on the tongue, and how sick it makes me.

The conclusion to the Skambraks story I was to experience some weeks later.

Misfortunes seldom come alone. Heinz and I were on detached duty at battalion HQ with two telephone linesmen. It gutted the adjutant that he could not put the regimental signals people on trench digging duty. We defended ourselves with our work and telephoned regiment to make them aware of what was afoot. They confirmed we did not have to do any digging: telecommunications had to be guaranteed at all times. How important we still were – almost proud of our indispensability to the regiment. We had just discussed this subject to our satisfaction when – hardly believing our eyes – we saw in the meagre light of our candles a face we all knew appear in the doorway.

It was Werner Zutraun, wearing the insignia of rank of an *Unteroffizier*. He was one of our best soldiers and wore the Iron Cross Second Class, Eastern Front Medal, and Infantry Assault Badge, but had been thrown out of the War Academy in Berlin. In a subdued voice he explained that he had had misfortune, and had been struck by bad luck. 'I have a Jewish grandparent and failed to disclose it in a sworn statement. So now I can't be an officer. It seems to me that I am a third-class person. I have to report to an infantry company. It was suggested to me that I should rehabilitate myself by distinguished conduct.'[3]

'But that is nonsense,' I said. It seemed that an infantry company was now actually a penal company for Skambraks and Zutraun. We took our leave of each other as we had always done and he joined the messenger waiting to lead him down the narrow log path to the company. We didn't talk much more that evening, everybody kept his thoughts to himself. 'It seems to me that I am a third-class person.' I can still hear him saying that with his slight lisp.

We never saw Werner Zutraun again. In the fighting south of Lake Ladoga in January 1943 he was shot in the stomach. In order not to weaken his company, he refused help from men of his squad who wanted to take him to the dressing station. He set off for there alone, and never arrived. Somewhere in the snowy desert of the frozen swamps his life of suffering ended. The great white shroud covered him over and only after the thaw in spring was he found, eaten by the rats.

We still have not yet reached the eventful year of 1943. We were able to celebrate a peaceful Christmas in 1942, the first time that the front allowed us to think of home. Along the main front line the Russians serenaded us with the most beautiful German Christmas carols and then their loudspeakers appealed to us to defect. They would go to any lengths to demoralise us.

Chapter 7 Notes

1. The term *Grabenstärke*, literally 'trench strength', meant that part of the unit directly facing the enemy, i.e. the main battle line without rearward services or *Tross*. *Trans.*
2. Probably a reference to Soldatensender Calais, a British black propaganda radio station widely listened to by German servicemen. Steiniger's memory seems to be faulty – he may well have listened to it, but not at this time since it only started broadcasting in November 1943. *Trans.*
3. Hitler's Army Adjutant, Major Gerhard Engel, described in his memoir how cases of partial Jewish ancestry in members of the Wehrmacht were dealt with, particularly the question whether a man could continue to serve. The case of a quarter-Jew (one Jewish grandparent) would be referred to Hitler personally, who judged the matter by looking at the man's photograph. Gerhard Engel: *At the Heart of the Reich: The Secret Diary of Hitler's Army Adjutant*, Greenhill Books, 2005. *Trans.*

CHAPTER 8

'P 5' and Height 43.3 – Sinyavino

EVERY GERMAN SOLDIER WHO FOUGHT south of Lake Ladoga knows the landmarks P 5, P 6, Height 43.3 – Sinyavino, Elektroschneise, Gleisdreieck, Geisterwald, Wenglerweg – all unforgettable names linked to the bitter fighting which went on here against an enemy greatly superior in numbers and materials. The American deliveries of weapons and food to the USSR had long since made their impact. Our U-boats could not stop this gigantic material assistance from the United States. Fighting at Lake Ladoga and near Leningrad very often demanded of our soldiers acts of great heroism in order to hold the front. The Russian T-34 tank, an outstanding medium battle tank with sloped armour, a good turn of speed, broad tracks and because of these manoeuvrability in swamplands, was greatly feared by our infantry, though not for long. Modern close-combat weapons such as the Panzerfaust, Panzerschreck (which we sometimes called the *Ofenrohr* ['Stovepipe'] and hollow-charge limpet mines soon found its weak spots, as did the Tiger tank, which we were to meet at P 5 for the first time. The battles in this latitude often gave rise to hopeless situations for our far weaker units or sections of them – yet despite that they could turn the tables.

On 12 January 1943 the Soviets launched a major offensive towards Lake Ladoga simultaneously from the west, therefore from Leningrad, and from the east. Following softening up by artillery, they attacked our sectors of the front, which reached to the shores of Lake Ladoga. On the first day they made great inroads into the German lines. Therefore our regiment was loaded into buses on 14 January and driven to the fray. The destination was the important rail junction in German hands at Mga. From afar we could hear the continuous booming from the front. The knowledge that that was where we had to go affected my stomach and mind, the naked fear for my life. Once I was in the midst of the fighting, however, this would give way to a feeling of nonchalant resignation, or at least so it was with me. The courageous, the valiant, thrilled other soldiers by their apparent cold-bloodedness and their initiatives against the attacking enemy. These were the real heroes, the essential steel framework of an intact army. I did not belong to this military elite. Recognising this fact did not depress me nor did it leave me particularly happy.

Our bus was peppered by shell splinters from artillery fire. On that 14 January German forces at Lake Ladoga had become encircled. On our arrival we found the battalions of our regiment already in action attempting to open a corridor through to their positions. We of the regimental signals platoon were unloaded and led to the front immediately. We had fine winter weather – not too cold, the sun gave the snowy landscape a soft, golden shimmer, only discoloured by heated powder from impacting shells. The next snowfall would soon cover it over. As we approached the battle area along a valley bottom, a fairly large swarm of Russian fighter-bombers came towards us.

Everybody lay flat but the enemy pilots ignored us, apparently having another set objective. From scarcely fifty metres away two twin flak guns took them under fire. We saw clearly how the 2-cm tracer rounds disappeared into their fuselages. Finally one of the machines tipped over, out of control, and then another. Two loud crashes, and black smoke rose from where the bombers hit the ground. A third machine began trailing a banner of smoke, then a little later spiralled down with motor howling. We were heartened by this show. Hats off to the 2-cm flak!

Our jubilation did not last long. A short time after we resumed our march in single infantry file we had to draw in our heads as small shells exploded amongst us. I guessed rifle grenades although I am still not sure that the Russians had them. Finally we got to 'P 5'. To build their railways, the Russians had had to erect dams in the swampy land. The workforce employed for that purpose was housed in workers' settlements called '*Rabochiy Poselok*'. P was short for *Poselok*, and the settlement number was added, hence 'P 5'.

At P 5, artillery had destroyed most of the brick houses. Our regimental command post was in the cellar of such a ruined house at the edge of the settlement and we of the regimental signals platoon were billeted nearby. Earth bunkers had been built at the centre of the village and the dressing station set up there. The bunkers were so hopelessly crammed with seriously wounded troops that the lightly wounded had to lie outside the entrances. This put a great strain on them, for the nights were bitterly cold. Directly in front of the regimental command post stood a Tiger tank, an impressive colossus which commanded respect. Unfortunately the type was not all that fast but by way of compensation had very good armour and an excellent 8.8-cm cannon. That was the situation when we arrived at P 5.

The new regimental leader was Major Krudzki, an impressive well-built man of sympathetic demeanour. Hauptmann Krieg his adjutant was smaller, blond and energetic. The long scars on his face might have been duelling scars from his student days. He was an experienced and proven company commander of open character; one sensed it from the first meeting with him.

We sat in the cellar awaiting the new day. Heinz Schimanski had left us to be battle-sketch artist at regimental HQ. At daybreak on 15 January Hans Weikert and I were ordered to follow the advance of the company of Oberleutnant Heckler, our former staff officer, with our radio apparatus so as to ensure the connection to regiment. The sun and temperature rose, and later the frost became milder. The advance proceeded with nothing unusual to report. Wherever one looked was endless snowy steppe. Where low bushes and thick undergrowth had managed to take hold, snowdrifts built up which offered unexpected protection, otherwise knee-deep snow lay everywhere. I trudged behind the advancing company, the heavy radio equipment on my back, my head drawn in. The weight of the casing forced my legs deeper into the snow: despite the cold I sweated. Frequently we passed dead Germans and Russians from previous encounters lying at peace just as they had fallen – now half or almost totally snowed over and frozen solid. Their yellowish hands and faces projected from the snow like limestone, covered by hoar frost.

Towards midday we reached a railway embankment. Oberleutnant Heckler told us to set up the radio equipment in the protection of the embankment and send the message: 'Reached railway embankment, no connection to neighbour left flank.' Above, on the edge of the embankment, a light machine gun had been installed, unfortunately a defective one unable to fire bursts. Whilst we were setting up the radio the machine gunner informed Oberleutnant Heckler that the Russians had crept up to the main battle line, then he returned and began firing at them with single rounds. Suddenly, without a sound, the gunner rolled down the embankment, almost to our feet, blood flowing from a small point of entry in his upper left cheekbone. He made some uncontrolled arm movements in the air and then his eyes remained open 'in surprise'.

Soldiers covered in dust gratefully accepting water and fruit brought up by village women in Estonia.

A reconnaissance patrol wearing field camouflage.

Soldiers of 162nd Infantry Regiment chatting with local girls somewhere in Estonia.

At the same moment excited shouting came from my left as our men abandoned their positions and came running down the embankment slope. As they ran off, Russians appeared on

the embankment and began firing their machine pistols freehand into the fleeing Germans. Heckler tried to save the situation, running after the fleeing men and shouting 'Back, the position must be held!' but the retreat was unstoppable. I had no time to pack up the radio equipment or demolish it. It stood set up and ready for use. The situation was plainly hopeless and now I ran too, as fast as the high snow would allow, leaving behind me the chaos and shouting wounded. I also saw nothing more of Hans Weikert. I stopped some distance away between snowdrifts to collect my thoughts and realised that I had no choice but to tell regiment about the Russian breakthrough.

Far to the rear, on the horizon in the north-west on a small elevation, I could see the chimneys of P 5. I set off towards them as fast as my legs would carry me and eventually arrived totally exhausted. 'Where have you come from?' Feldwebel Hofer asked me with surprise, 'We have been calling you consistently but got no answer.'

'The Russians broke through. There was total confusion. Our front has collapsed.'

He turned pale and disappeared at once from the bunker, re-appearing a short while afterwards to escort me to the command post. I saluted on entering and saw alongside Major Krudzki a general, our divisional commander General Hühner, who had come personally to be advised on the situation. Krudzki to me: 'Now, tell me calmly. What have you seen?' I explained that we reached the railway embankment without difficulty, and that suddenly the main front line was rolled up on our left flank, at which our men retreated in disorder.

Krudzki: 'Can you read a map?'

'I believe so, sir.'

'Here is the embankment which you had reached. Where did the Russians come from?'

'Most of them from here at the left.'

Major Krudzki turned to the general. 'It is as I assumed, Herr General, there was a large gap not of our making between ourselves and our neighbour on the left flank.' At that I was dismissed.

Meanwhile the Russians had got between us and our rearward connections to the south and were now pushing forward to the west. A reconnaissance troop brought the confirmation – we were encircled. Encircled without reserves or provisions. A thin defensive front line was set up ahead of the regimental command post facing south. The telephone connection to division had remained intact: the Russians had overlooked it under the snow.

Through this connection we received instructions to hold out, Tiger tanks were to make an attack to free us. Nevertheless the mood was one of depression. Above all the situation for the wounded was intolerable. The medical orderlies put together a train of all available sledges and horses for the wounded. Since it was snowing, it was hoped they could find a gap and slip through the enemy lines. It was a very long train which disappeared into the blizzard.

P 5 lay under artillery and tank fire. We had not eaten for two days and we had little ammunition. Then the weather improved giving us some hope of supply from the air. In the evening aircraft came, but not many; we could see their shadowy outlines against the starry sky. Some of the supply containers fell behind the Russian lines, we ourselves got nothing since the infantry companies were more needy.

By 17 January 1943 the hoped-for liberation by the Tigers had still not come. I had not eaten for three days, my last can of fish was in my radio pack. We were exhausted and nervous, chain-smoking endlessly, huddled together in the bunkers. Our lethargy was broken by the shout, 'Everybody out, Russian tanks are attacking!' We split up between the medical bunkers shouting '*Hurra! Hurra!*' and fired at anybody moving at the eastern entrance. Our own Tiger prepared for action. It had little fuel and was immobile, but had just enough in its tanks to turn the turret. With the few armour-piercing shells still remaining it fired at one of the many Russian tanks which had already passed the village entrance. One round from the Tiger – a Russian tank blazed. The second round – another one destroyed. The Russians spotted our Tiger and hit it. Sparks a metre long sprayed from the steel of the armoured cupola but no hit penetrated. A young panzer lieutenant stood on the roof of one of the medical bunkers, upright as a candle, directing the fire of his Tiger. Every round fired meant one Russian tank less. After they had lost eight tanks they broke off the attack and withdrew. Our '*Hurra!*' came from weakened bodies but uplifted hearts. Our defensive victory meant nothing but our survival.

Our end seemed to have been postponed and at about 0130 hrs on the morning of 18 January 1943 the order came to break out and proceed to the German lines towards P 6, Sinyavino. In the early hours we set off in two groups. Major Krudzki led one group; the second, of which I formed part, was under the command of Hauptmann Krieg. He led it from the front, machine pistol at the ready. The operation began in full darkness. We cannot have got far from P 5 before coming to a standstill to find cover. Two Russian light tanks held us up. The ice of the swamp had given way under their weight and they were a quarter sunk but their crews could still fire their machine guns. Left of me lay Oberleutnant Kopp from Tilsit who had been awarded the Knight's Cross for his part in the encirclement battle at the Volkhov. He was dead. It was almost dawn before we could continue. Exhausted and famished, calling on our last reserves of strength in knee-high

An abandoned Russian position with its barbed wire defences.

snow, we plodded onwards to the south. Whoever couldn't keep up here would die. Our advance continued without any further interruption from the enemy and we passed through the first Russian lines.

The worst experience for me was still ahead. It was already daylight. Rather to one side of the main body we came to a slightly hilly region. Strewn over a large area were dead horses, overturned sledges, and between them German dead and wounded, the medical transport which had left P 5. 'Comrade, take me with you,' a weak voice implored me from a bundle of field grey uniform and bandages lying in the snow. The survivors were begging us for their lives, begging us who were ourselves at the end of our strength. If only one of them at least could hobble on one leg!

But carry them? We tore ourselves away knowing that they were certain to die. They could choose: freeze to death or be killed by the Russians when they caught up. To be the last glimmer of hope for these poor men and yet have to pass them by gave me a feeling of guilt, as if we were their killers. I still bear the burden today. But what purpose would it have served to sacrifice my own life in the hopeless attempt to save theirs?

The advance faltered again. Under infantry fire we threw ourselves down in the snow. The snow in front of me sprayed up for a few seconds, and then from behind a snowdrift appeared four

The fate of heroes: Gefreiter Paul Heinz and Gefreiter Georg Baumgart fell during an artillery bombardment near Potsamaa in July 1941.

raised hands. Two Russians approached us uncertainly. The size of the group at our rear may have prompted their decision. Now they plodded along with us and we took no notice of them, we had quite enough to do already, for a fresh tragic situation now began.

Well-aimed artillery fire arrived from the south. 'That can only be German guns! They think we're Russians and are dropping barrier fire!' It almost seemed as though our people at P 6 intended to finish what the Russians had not been able to do at P 5. The shooting was devastatingly accurate. I was lucky and found cover in a fork of the railway embankment. The shells either exploded on the embankment above and the splinter effect passed overhead, or twenty to thirty metres behind me, most of it continuing in the direction of fire. Bubi Büchs lay near me. The terrible minutes passed until finally the gunners saw our flares and recognised us as German. It seemed that the SS-Polizei at P-6 had not been informed of our break-out. Most of our casualties were now due to friendly fire. Major Krudzki was seriously wounded. When they lifted him up, he ordered them to hand him his pistol. His last words were reported to be, 'Tell my wife and daughter that I died a good death.' I was not present, being with Group Krieg. The *Major* knew his men well. Either he did not want them to feel under any obligation or he knew that his wound was not survivable.

Far behind us in open country, Russian artillery was now in position. The land was flat and lacked cover as far as the naked eye

Morning mist clearing after a night spent under canvas in open country.

could see. The two Russians who had 'attached' themselves to us took the opportunity to slip away when the first shells arrived in and around P 6. Brown powder-smoke arose. The Russians were firing at our artillery, not at us.

We left the danger zone and reached our own lines at P 6. A rider, mounted on horseback, trotted past me with a nod which

The regimental command position in an Estonian farmyard during the advance in 1941: Generalleutnant Siegfried Haenicke, commander 61st Infantry Division (sitting at table): Oberst Walter Melzer, commander 151st Infantry Regiment (sitting by wall holding telephone receiver), Oberleutnant Rapreger, Hauptmann Dr Pankow and Leutnant Heckler.

said everything. Long, blond stringy hair hung over the rider's ears, the yellowish-grey sky reflected in the goggles of his gas mask: it could only be Ernst Skambraks, one foot heavily bandaged. His horse was towing a Finnish kayak with a wounded man. For Ernst the war was over. His last act for the German Wehrmacht was to retrieve a wounded man, and the horse saved them both.

Thus ended the P 5 operation. Filthy and with the beginnings of a beard I arrived near the field kitchen of a *Gebirgsjäger* company. The first ladleful of warm soup was heavenly beyond description and warmed my whole body. The cook was probably running no risk in serving men from another unit, for the numbers collecting their entitlement to rations in his own company were constantly dwindling.

The regimental signals platoon assembled in an old bunker behind the artillery emplacements. A bucket of warm water stood in the centre of the room for washing and shaving. The colour and consistency of the soapy water after everybody had washed and shaved in it can be imagined. I was hoping that we would be granted a few days to rest and recover, but the *Tross* collected up all rifles from returners for a fresh issue and in the event we had only one day's rest.

Next day, 20 January 1943, we occupied a prepared position at Height 43.3. Between batteries of mortars and artillery we found ourselves an old artillery ammunition bunker. The floor was frozen water. We crouched down and froze too, listening to our mortar batteries firing their deafening salvoes. This was terrific for our morale. After firing there would be a light rustling noise in the air and then a fine whistling as the mortar bombs flew towards the enemy to explode in a broad wall of fire and black smoke. Mortar fire like this is impressive: the Russians knew that our 'fortress' was bristling with artillery of various descriptions and took it under fire with help from their fighter-bombers.

We awaited our orders. Night fell. We found a round iron stove and two sacks of charcoal, stood the stove in the centre of the room and got the little fire glowing. It radiated such warmth that even the men sitting on the plank beds under the bunker roof found it warm there. The entrance hole into the bunker was covered by a blanket to trap the heat. Almost simultaneously those on the plank beds began to complain of headaches and nausea. Erich Schubert began to spout nonsense and broke into tuneless song. Carbon monoxide poisoning! We laid him out in the fresh air in front of the bunker. He began to freeze, had some more 'enlightening moments' and crept back into the warmth. The game began again. Bubi Büchs and I carried Erich outside once more.

The area was under almost continuous artillery fire and I did not hear the shell coming. Suddenly I was hit at the base of the spine by what felt like a clod of earth. Then I felt the blood running from where the shell splinter had hit me. I could still move my legs which was the main thing. At the dressing station in a nearby blockhouse I was given a 'wounded' label, a dressing and a tetanus jab. Then I resumed my place at the oven waiting for the sled which would take me behind the lines. Theo Rösler, who had a bout of jaundice, gave me a grin as if to say, 'Boy, are we lucky!'

Very early next morning, once I was bedded on hay on the sled, the driver whipped the horse into motion to get us clear of artillery range as quickly as possible, and at Kelkolovo we were safe apparently. Field Hospital 508 Volossovo was the final station. It lay in Russian territory about seventy kilometres short of Narva. A Viennese surgeon examined me, dictated his diagnosis, had me gyrate both my legs and then told me how lucky I had been, a few more millimetres and it could have left me paraplegic. As a result of the unfavourable resting place of the artillery splinter between the nerve endings, he decided not to operate. After draining off the pus, the splinter, the size of a finger nail, encapsulated and I still have it inside me as a memento of that 20 January 1943 day. My five-week stay in hospital passed quietly apart from two bombing raids on Volossovo and the nightly mosquitoes and bugs. The

Break-time: Leutnant Baltruschat and his sergeant of 1st Battalion, 151st Infantry Regiment, Estonia 1941.

nurses complained that the cockroaches sated themselves at night on ichthyol salve in the bandaging room.

During my period in hospital the tragedy at Stalingrad came to its end. I thought how small was my own experience compared to what those soldiers went through there. In the course of time I learned to interpret the Wehrmacht bulletins and translate them

into the human military catastrophes which would affect countless thousands. There is no greater misfortune for humanity than war.

At the end of the five weeks I was sent to the Convalescent Company at Riga for fourteen days and then returned to the signals platoon by local trains. The regiment was awaiting spring at a quiet, beautifully swampy location. Accommodation was earth bunkers or blockhouses but at least we were not under fire from artillery. We cultivated friendships, did light duties and the members of our band, who in action served at the front as paramedics, medical orderlies and stretcher bearers, got their instruments back. They had a wide repertoire from the regimental march to popular melodies.

In the spring of 1943 the Russians bombarded us with leaflets about their victory at Stalingrad. The number 330,000 crossed through appeared on the front of the leaflet and below it the number 90,000, the total of Sixth Army men going into Soviet captivity of whom only about 7,000 would ever get home. Later more leaflets were dropped with headings and photographs of the 'Freies Deutschland Kommittee' begun by Erich Steinert and General von Seydlitz and a message. These leaflets always bore Stalin's quote: 'The Hitlers come and go, the German people remain.' One of these leaflets was a particular favourite of mine. On the left an athletic Russian stripped to the waist rubbing snow over his arms and chest, brimming with health. Beside him on the right, chilled to the marrow, head drawn in, thick ear muffs, snot running from his nose – in short a picture of misery – a German soldier. Below the photos the caption ran: 'What is healthy for the Russian is ruin for the German.' All leaflets contained a printed authorisation for would-be defectors to cross the Russian lines.

At this time in the spring of 1943 I celebrated the first anniversary of my pen-friendship with the Tilsit girl I had never met. Our exchange of letters had become very personal and passed the limits of 'just a pen-friendship'. Now and again she would send me a small book, generally a novel, and the very precise way she packed the field parcel helped me gain an impression of her character. In her letters she was concerned for me when heavy fighting was reported in our section of the front. Her only brother Heinz, of whom she was very fond, a lieutenant with the infantry, had been missing since Stalingrad (and never came home subsequently). Her letters were a fixed component of my life as a soldier and I looked forward to them very much.

CHAPTER 9

The Kirishi Bridgehead

IN ABOUT MID-MAY 1943 we came to the Kirishi bridgehead on the eastern bank of the Volkhov on a railway line to Leningrad. Since the German advance in the late autumn of 1941 the area had not been intended for any particular purpose and allowed to wither. During the defensive fighting earlier it had been razed to the ground. Of the village itself nothing remained, not even the chimneys. Our companies had now settled in the remaining cellars. The entire bridgehead extended about two kilometres along the river bank and was one kilometre deep. Its worst feature was its total exposure to enemy surveillance, which made it a paradise for snipers. The Wehrmacht retaliated with its own snipers.

The symbol of Kirishi was its bridge over the Volkhov, however. Our regimental command post, in a cutting in the railway embankment, was not far from this arched railway bridge. The bridge was several hundred metres long and had been damaged by explosives at each end so that those parts of its steel structure drooped into the river. Above the waterline the gaps had been bridged with wooden beams and boards to make it reasonably passable for foot traffic. At night all the supplies passed this way and so it came under almost constant nuisance fire. Everybody who had to cross it in daylight needed to use all those techniques of gait and pace imaginable which the situation demanded. During my stay at Kirishi I had to cross it six times, three times there and back. Our telephone linesmen went across more frequently, for no matter how carefully the lines were laid they were always prone to splinter damage. The linesmen would then have to sit on the bridge attempting to find the right ends amongst the tangles

The Alexander Nevski Cathedral at Reval (Tallinn).

of wiring and if successful patch them together again. Often linesmen from the artillery and divisional HQ would come for the same purpose. The sound of the steel framework of the bridge vibrating when it received a direct hit became as familiar to us as the chiming of the clocks back home.

Obviously field kitchens and rations-carriers had no place here. Therefore on both sides of the bridge, the catering provided was meals in tins to be warmed up and served as and when required and would perhaps be beans with bacon, peas and lentils with smoked meats, or rice and cabbage with beef, plus some cold rations and other items. These supplies, ammunition and equipment had to be delivered over the bridge by night under enemy artillery fire and the responsibility fell to men of Penal Battalion 500, any commentary here being superfluous.

Our new regimental commander was Oberst Müller-Melahn from Tilsit, and his adjutant, whom I knew from the earlier days of my service, was Hermann Schumacher, later at divisional HQ. One day, together with Bubi Büchs, I was summoned to the presence of the *Herr Oberst*. He had a vigorous manner about him and was not shy about publicity, his initials 'M-M' appeared on all the regiment's tactical signs so that the regimental command post could always be found without making enquiries. The occasion was my award of the Iron Cross Second Class: I was the first man in the regiment to receive the award from him since his arrival. 'Do you know what it's for?' he asked. Still overcome by the honour, I thought back and could find nothing I had done at Kirishi which would have merited it.

'For P 5,' the *Oberst* explained, 'for coming back to inform the regiment of the Russian breakthrough.' The award completed my collection, for it confirmed me as a veteran of the Russian Front – a '*Frontschwein*' – from the lower ranks. I had the Ostmedaille, Infantry Assault Badge, Wound Badge in Black and now the Iron Cross Second Class. For the coveted Close Combat Clasp I had thirteen verified close-combat days, and by the summer of 1944,

A college at Reval, Estonia.

after further service, I was still two days short of the requirement to qualify. However, I was not totally committed to getting those two days, and that may be why I survived. One should not interfere with the spokes of one's personal wheel of destiny!

At Kirishi I was given a new kind of job temporarily. Heinz Schimanski had gone on leave and suggested me as his deputy

battle-sketch artist. This job entailed collecting statements from the battalions in the early morning regarding the events of the previous night such as casualty reports, trench strengths and anything unusual, and assembling them for immediate presentation to the adjutant. Despite the very quiet front there were daily dead and wounded at the hands of the accursed snipers. My main task was to sketch in on tracing paper true to scale and in various colours the entire course of progress of the bridgehead front with all weapons down to machine guns and all changes on the German side, and also the known Russian installations and their equipment with weaponry. A curiosity was the designation 'brothel bunker'. The Russians actually had women in the front line 'to attend to the needs of the troops'. On mild summer evenings we could hear music on an accordion and the various noises made by the women.

I liked the job of battle-sketcher, it was interesting and informative. What did not please me about Kirishi was the knowledge that I was at a small bridgehead across a river several hundred metres wide and I couldn't swim. On one of their attacks in 1942, the Russians had almost reached the Volkhov bridge. What else was unpleasant about Kirishi? The plague of mosquitoes and the relatively rare but always impressive large-calibre rocket bombardments aimed at the regimental command post. They were said to be of American origin. None of our bunker huts was hit during my presence there, however.

CHAPTER 10

Pogarelushka

THERE WAS LITTLE HEAVY FIGHTING in this period and we were either used as reserves for the possibility of an attempt by the Russians to lift the siege of Leningrad during the summer, or were simply being rested for a few days. The regimental HQ and the companies now had quarters in a long village called Pogarelushka a few kilometres from the big railway junction at Mga. The wooden houses were free of vermin, the weather continued fine and we were in good spirits. Now and again the Russian artillery would fire a salvo at Mga, which would pass overhead on the way to the railway station, or perhaps to the gigantic railway gun stationed there.

The Russians had an artillery spotter sitting in the basket of a tethered balloon from where he could undoubtedly see into our village clearly. If the Luftwaffe appeared the balloon would be pulled down immediately and rise again once they had gone. As a precaution we dug slit trenches, in a zig-zag line as per the manual, behind our houses. Our signals vehicles were parked in the shadows and well camouflaged.

Parallel to the road through our village about 100 metres off was a brook lined by alders so that its course was exactly marked. Suddenly a shell exploded close to the brook and then some time later a second one. These rounds presented us with no danger but puzzled us by their purpose. Next day we had the finest weather again. I was polishing my boots on the doorstep, Feldwebel Hofer had tuned in the short-wave receiver to a concert on the Soldatensender frequency. Suddenly shells came hissing down from a clear blue sky to explode in the centre of the village road

A Mark IV panzer followed by a Mark III, heading towards Leningrad. The picture was taken during the first autumn of the campaign, as can be seen by the tank crew's greatcoats. It was much colder where they were going!

Reval burning, August 1941.

and amongst our neighbouring houses. An artillery barrage on Pogarelushka!

I joined Hofer in a slit trench, and when our own house was hit I waited for the few seconds pause for 'our battery' to reload, left the trench and sprinted across the meadow to the railway embankment where there were bunkers and stables. The bombardment lasted

no more than ten minutes. Pogarelushka was in flames, horses lay dead or injured and in distress. These had to be given the *coup de grâce.*

Great excitement in the regimental signals platoon: Wolfgang von Ulardt had begun pushing the signals' waggons away from the tremendous heat of the fires, having realised the risk of the hollow charge limpet mines in every waggon being set off. He yelled at everybody, including those senior in rank, 'Get away, quick!' And they obeyed. The waggons with all our equipment were saved by his brave action. Besides the horses, the artillery bombardment had caused dead and wounded amongst the companies although our platoon had been lucky and nobody was hurt.

In August 1943 it seemed likely that the Russians were bound to prepare a new offensive to liberate Leningrad, especially since the battles of the previous winter had gained for them a nine-kilometre-wide land connection south of Lake Ladoga. Our battalions were now being thrown into the fray. It was decided that members of the signals platoon should proceed to the Luga area to engage partisans. This was an operation to smoke out a partisan base on a sandy island in the swamps. Something new again! The district was one of low hills interspersed with swampy woodlands and there was a small lake. In the evening I attended a dance with the young people of the village. I went with Werner Haferbier and several others. We lined up with the folk dancers and stamped together with the Russians while the walls and floor reverberated. Partisans might have been watching this foolishness from the edge of the village or inside it, but we did not give them a thought until we got back to our quarters and realised then how reckless and light-headed we had been.

Next day, with our radio equipment, Werner and I were attached to an anti-partisan squad. With the *Unteroffizier* in charge it consisted of three Germans, the rest all being members of the 'Russian Liberation Army' our leaders had set up. We set out cautiously – the partisans liked to put landmines along the paths and so we trod with care. Our route led across wet, swampy forest glades and woodland paths until finally we came to a brook where we were to spend the night. We three Germans shared a tent. Our Russians had gone fishing with hand grenades in the brook, which would certainly have alerted any partisans to our presence and so guaranteed us a quiet night. It would have been about 2200 hrs when suddenly we were awoken from sleep by a loud crackling. The *Unteroffizier* jumped up, burst through the closed flap of the tent collapsing it over Werner and myself and stood with his Schmeisser at the ready, looking at the brightly burning fire the Russians had built and for which even now they were chopping wood to keep it going all night. The partisans could therefore not stumble across us by accident, and perhaps this had been the purpose of the fire. In any case, I freely admit that I was not too upset about it.

Next day we returned having made no contact with the enemy. The assault troop part of the operation had been a wash-out. When they reached the sandy island and found the partisans' bunkers, the birds had flown. They must have slipped through the German lines in the morning mist. We were returned to the still quiet front at Lake Ladoga. Here at least we knew who was friend and foe. I was offered and accepted October for my third spell of home leave, which was to have a decisive effect on my later life.

On my arrival I found the mood in Germany and my Sudeten homeland to be one of confidence in victory but subdued. I could

Members of the regimental staff look at burning Reval from a gymnasium at a safe distance from the fighting. In the picture are Oberfeldwebel Pawlzig and Feldwebel Noack.

not answer the enquiries of my old work colleagues at the Bilin warehouse optimistically with a clear conscience. The warehouse director told me ironically: 'Just wait, the *Wunderwaffe* – the Miracle Weapon – is coming soon!' The aged, industrious book-keeper Knobloch, my previous immediate superior, alluding to innuendos that the war was already lost, asked, 'What will become of us Sudeten Germans then?' I could not offer him an answer. He was probably thinking of the return of the fanatical Czechs . . .

My leave ended all too soon, and 21 November 1943 found me on the train to Tilsit via Dresden. It pulled into Tilsit at 1400 hrs and now I found myself at a loose end since I did not have to report to the Front Direction Office at Pogegen until 2000 hrs. I stowed my rifle at the left-luggage office and then headed for the phone exchange intending to present myself to my unknown female pen-friend. A lady at the telegraph office regretted very much that Fräulein N. was off duty today and at home. She told me how to get to Grünwalder Strasse and I set off in a state of nerves. I passed some bombed-out houses – a few days previously Tilsit had been bombed for the first time – and after an uphill walk I found No. 3 and pressed the bell. Nothing stirred. After the second attempt I rang the bell for the housekeeper to leave a message that I had called. 'Such bad luck,' she said, 'Mother and daughter are always at home but today they had to order a wreath for a relative who died. You can wait with me if you like, come in.' I accepted the invitation and now I learned everything worth knowing: what a good family they were, that they had lived here for fifteen years, the daughter (my pen-friend) was such a nice girl, her elder sister was a student and the second one had married well.

At 1700 hrs I had to take my leave; outside in blacked-out Tilsit it was already pitch-dark. I had walked scarcely thirty steps when behind me the door of No. 3 Grünwalder Strasse was torn open and a lively, bright voice called my name. I heard hasty female footsteps, then an arm was thrust through mine, and I was taken to meet my future mother-in-law.

Scarcely had the Soviets been driven out than Estonian men and women laid wreaths on the Estonian peace memorial.

The first meeting with my pen-friend lasted a good hour, and she decided our future. She was much prettier in person than in the photos of herself she had sent me, and had a winning manner. On the way to Tilsit station I asked if she had thought that we might use the informal pronoun '*Du*' instead of '*Sie*' in our letters . . . from then on we were silent, both knowing we had met our future marriage partner. I left wearing a small amber heart around my neck, the sign of everlasting love.

When I returned to my unit on 25 November 1943 in the railway triangle at Mga, I was told that during my leave a number of strong but locally limited attacks by the Russians had been repulsed. The front had fallen quiet again and we could hope to celebrate Christmas undisturbed. What I remember of those pre-Christmas days are the large rats which ran around the command post between the bunkers. The corpses of the fallen from the fighting over the foregoing weeks had been gathered up and stored here at our command post prior to being taken to the military cemeteries. The rats were active around these corpses at night. If one lit a pocket torch in the pitch dark, one would get a shock if the beam of light shone suddenly into a hollow skull where only stringy tufts of hair remained of an almost completed process of decomposition. Large and fat, like cats, the rats sat between the dead. Their eyes lit up ghostly and phosphorescent when the light struck them. They would make no attempt to run off, they were too gorged and too lazy. It filled me with horror.

CHAPTER 11

The Last Battle For Leningrad

Leningrad could normally be accessed by sea via the Gulf of Finland. Now the northern shore was either Finnish territory or held by the Finns and the southern shore between Estonia and the outskirts of Leningrad was occupied by German forces except for the Oranienbaum Pocket. This was a coastal enclave roughly 30 km wide and 16 km deep, which remained under Soviet control throughout the siege of Leningrad from September 1941 onwards. At the centre of the pocket was the Krasnaya Gorka fort complex. In September 1943, the Soviet High Command decided that if the Germans did not withdraw during the next two months they would implement a plan to lift the siege of Leningrad based on their foothold in the Oranienbaum pocket. Accordingly, from early November 1943, the Soviets began secretly transporting thousands of troops and huge quantities of guns and tanks to the enclave by night. On 14 January 1944 supported by warships of the Baltic Fleet, and artillery on the offshore island and naval base of Kronstadt, also never captured by German forces, 2nd Shock Army broke out from the Oranienbaum pocket to initiate the lifting of the siege.

THE CHRISTMAS LULL did not deceive me into believing that the winter offensive was not coming. When it did come, the location chosen by the Russians for their breakthrough was the Oranienbaum Pocket near where the former sanatorium had been. We had only the inexperienced 9th and 10th Luftwaffe Divisions deployed along the semi-circular land perimeter.

We had arrived near Oranienbaum and spent the night in solid concrete bunkers. Looking east from there one could see the

The arrival of German infantry in Reval at the end of August 1941, where life is apparently continuing as normal.

suburbs of Leningrad and a lighthouse with a flashing light. The only thing certain about 14 January 1944 which I remember, the most difficult rearguard action our regiment had ever had to face, is of our infantry companies being surprised by tanks coming at them from all sides most unexpectedly, and suffering very heavy

losses. Bubi Büchs fell and Werner Zahn is missing since then. I have no memory of what happened to my radio apparatus.

My ability to recall the early stages of that retreat is not good. Our weak lines had been overrun suddenly by strong tank forces and now we marched – if that is the correct word – in an endless crowd of troop members ranging from clerks to *Tross* operatives, infantry companies, signals people, messengers and so on in a direction which was roughly west. However I do recall Feldwebel Noack of the regimental office. He was normally a very calm person, unhurried and had a deliberate way of speaking. We had come under artillery fire and I found myself running in search of cover with him. There must have been a sporting side to his nature of which I was unaware for he could run at double-quick pace and I found it difficult to keep up. We were heading up a hill with two tanks behind us and got to the brow before they had a chance to bring their guns to bear. In those seconds we found a place on the elevation which was a blind spot for their gunners.

Our regimental staff gathered next day in a massive building resembling a castle to organise the next line of defence. Lacking my radio equipment I had to take ammunition forward on a sledge assisted by a *Hiwi* [Russian prisoner-volunteer]. I sat with him on the cases. The weather was fine and sunny. Trotting ahead of the sledge was a small but tough Russian horse of the steppe. It was no great distance, for the company command post was located in a small farmhouse not far from the 'castle'. I was surprised to be

approached by the former Gefreiter Hegele of the 2nd Battalion signals staff, the close-combat specialist of Nevabogen, now an officer and company commander. When he saw my reaction to his promotion he gave me a friendly grin while maintaining his distance as an officer. Before either of us had the chance to speak, there were multiple whistling noises in the air and then explosions all around had us diving into a nearby haystack. Almost at once another salvo followed, and this time the Stalin rockets were so close that we felt the air pressure of the explosions on our eardrums. Leutnant Hegele, the *Hiwi* and I were uninjured but the little horse was trembling over its whole body. It was not wounded, but shocked and frightened as we were. My Russki and I unloaded the ammunition boxes as fast as we could, and I paid my respects to Leutnant Hegele fairly rapidly. I never saw him again. He was reported missing next day. When I returned to the 'castle', it no longer had window panes, the Stalin-organ rockets had seen to that.

Next day the regimental HQ was pulled back to the rear. Major Brzoska, 2nd Battalion commander, fell that day. The new command post was set up to the north of a village, probably Kipen, in a house in its own grounds. The Leningrad–Narva *Rollbahn* passed at the south end of the village. The rearward services of all units rolled past here heading west, and we would be following them next day since we had no unit to support in the region.

A Wehrmacht loudspeaker van informing the Estonian civilian population of the situation in Reval.

Oberst Müller-Melahn was in occupation of the house which overlooked a plain jutting to the west. Very well camouflaged in front of the entrance to the house were two anti-tank guns, one each of 3.7-cm and 5-cm calibre. It was sunny, as usual for the

162nd Infantry Regiment graves at the edge of a wood.

A double grave between two telegraph poles in Estonia.

season, tolerably cold and visibility was good. From the western edge of vision, between the plain and the wood, a string of T-34 tanks came rolling in line ahead. We counted seventeen, and could see that if they continued on that course they would meet the retreating *Tross*. We had no radio and looked on helplessly. Suddenly one veered towards us as if to investigate, front profile heading straight for our house. The *Herr Oberst* gave his orders thoughtfully and warned us to keep quiet. 'Just don't panic,' was his advice. We left the house by the back way, and at its rear watched the tank from the shadows. The T-34 had crossed the plain, its motor becoming more audible every second. If we did not succeed in destroying the tank it would crash through the house and hunt us down across the flat plain with its machine guns. Why didn't the anti-tank guns fire? The tank was scarcely twenty metres from the house when the 5-cm gun fired, hitting the commander's cupola and jamming it. Then the stick-grenade fired by our 3.7-cm gun swept the turret away behind the tank to lie in the snow. The only survivor, a warrant officer radio operator, was unhurt and surrendered. We took him prisoner into the house. He was hefty and well-fed, nothing like the Russian soldiers of two winters earlier. Bubi Müller, our ordnance technician, did not think it safe to enter a burning, damaged tank to plant explosives to destroy it, and so the T-34 was left to burn out and could be seen still smouldering when night fell.

A section of the regimental signals platoon was deployed in the infantry role that evening. Unteroffizier Dreihsen took over the seven-man group, its other six members being Wolfgang, Pat Wachnowski, Arnold Mathäus, Hans Kreiner, Bubi Reimann and myself. We were given guard duty until midnight when we could stand down. All we saw in the snowy fields was the odd cat, otherwise nothing to report except stray infantry fire coming our way from the rear.

Bubi Reimann was then sent to the command post for ammunition because the supply seemed too short for what we

Estonian civilians in conversation at the wayside apparently glad that the Soviet occupation is over. Their hopes of more independence were not fulfilled by the Germans.

might have to face later. The regimental HQ had been shifted that evening and only one staff officer, Leutnant Zacher, was present. When he returned, Bubi said he had heard some tank noises coming

from the village and thought he heard people shouting 'Panzerfaust! Panzerfaust!' He alerted the sentry to this and then tramped through the snow to Leutnant Zacher's room. The other two rooms were full of sleeping infantrymen, amongst them the two crews of our successful anti-tank guns. When Bubi informed the lieutenant of what he had heard, Leutnant Zacher didn't think it very serious and said it was most likely armoured troop-carriers of the SS Division *Nordland* in the village.

That same moment there was a tremendous crash, the sound of splintering, cries – the candle fell down, leaving the room in total darkness, the door jammed, dust and earth filled the room. Shouting and groans came from the collapsed adjoining room. As a signals man, Bubi Reimann had a pocket lamp which he used to smash the window which he and Leutnant Zacher then jumped through. As they did so they saw a T-34 moving away.

This tank was one of the seventeen we had seen rolling along the edge of the plain earlier. It had likely fired off all its ammunition and, while returning to the Russian lines, its commander had decided to ram anything that moved. He must have seen a light in the house and have driven straight for it, bringing down the house and crushing the soldiers all crammed together inside sleeping. There were few survivors. The men died either mangled by the tank tracks or by falling beams. Amongst the victims were our valiant anti-tank gunners. They had not survived their triumph for long. Next the T-34 had gone through a barn occupied by Waffen-SS men, some of whom were struck by falling beams.

Upon his return, Bubi began his report to us, 'What I have just experienced . . .' and related what I have just described without any exaggeration. A soldier in war has to be lucky if he is to survive, and once again I had had luck on my side. If we had not been given infantry duty that night, we would now be lying amongst the other crushed bodies in the debris of that collapsed house.

At midnight, our seven-man squad pulled out and followed wherever the others were heading. None of it looked like an orderly retreat. The staffs do the wrong thing without troops to manage and the remnants of the former fighting units had lost their leaders. 'Save yourself who can!' was the cry. These last ten days of January were calamitous, for the retreat decomposed into wild, disorganised flight. For the first time we had an impression of how the great retreats of Army Groups Centre and South must have looked. I found it difficult to imagine how this crowd of dazed refugees could be re-assembled into a well-organised defensive unit unless fresh forces arrived to establish an interception line. Since there were no fresh forces, it seemed certain that Eighteenth Army was going to be wiped out.

Walther Hubatsch wrote about these last ten days of January 1944 in his oft-quoted history of 61st Infantry Division: 'Only with the greatest difficulty did we succeed in erecting a provisional barrier line from the remnants of 61st Division which survived the struggle against a force tenfold superior in numbers.' A few lines later he continued: 'In the evening, the Russian artillery shot the occupied villages into flames causing panic; foreign units, amongst them countless rearward services and *Tross* which had slipped from their commanders' grasp, trucks full of soldiers, stragglers and staffs without troops to control all pushed westward, more a running away than a planned withdrawal. The roads in the rearward area were blocked with traffic but the woods were empty of enemy.'

Generalleutnant Siegfried Haenicke, commander, 61st Infantry Division, wearing his Knight's Cross and his WWI Pour le Mérite.

The battalion commanders of 151st Infantry Regiment in discussion. From the left, Hauptmann Rooch, Hauptmann Dr Werner Pankow and Leutnant Dr Hubatsch.

It was precisely this situation which prompted us seven men of the regimental signals platoon to pledge to each other that we would remain together at all costs until we regained the regiment. There is nothing worse for a soldier than to be tossed into a heap not his own and which he does not know. The fear of being

abandoned while wounded is primarily responsible for the poor fighting value of such 'fire brigade units'. It was therefore agreed between Unteroffizier Dreihsen and his six men that we would stick together. No man of the seven being wounded would be left behind.

At night we came to Volossovo, the place I had been pushed into to be treated for my wound. The village was deserted. All the large wooden houses had been evacuated. We had gone several days without rations and were looking for anything edible. In a large room of one the houses we struck lucky and found piles of well-filled field packs. They had probably belonged to returners from leave who had been taken off the train in which they had just come from Germany, had been told to leave their packs in the heap and then sent straight into action. Whatever had happened to them they would not be returning here and eventually the Russians would benefit from the field packs. Therefore we took from every pack what we required urgently – food. I got two large tins and a loaf of bread. Unfortunately one of the tins contained only whole asparagus, certainly very good for me but in my situation pork would have been preferable. The other tin contained home-made liver sausage which kept me going for several days.

I seem to remember passing the tsarist castle at Krasnoye Selo and eventually joining the queue of rearward services and *Tross* at Kingisepp. Opposite us we saw parked the VW amphibious car of our regimental commanding officer. The *Herr Oberst* and

Major Dr Werner Pankow wearing the Knight's Cross awarded on 20 September 1941, when he was commanding 2nd Battalion, 151st Infantry Regiment.

Hauptmann Schumacher noticed us: 'Dreihsen, where have you come from?' the adjutant asked, pleasantly surprised but at the same time obviously having to wrestle with a problem which our appearance had caused him. Dreihsen made his report and after a while came back to us with a satisfied expression. 'We've done it!' he said, flourishing a document bearing the official stamp and signature of Oberst Müller-Melahn. It read: 'Unteroffizier Fritz Dreihsen is hereby ordered to proceed immediately with six men to Jõhvi in Estonia for the reorganisation of Grenadier-Regiment 151.' Thank God we now had a valid order, we were no longer shirkers and could make our way to the Narva with our heads held high.

In the evening we came to a Red Cross post and stopped for a serving of oatmeal soup, our first hot meal for ten days. The reason why I recall this incident particularly was for the nursing sister who ladled it out. She was of middle age, well built and very resolute. With every ladleful she would insult the soldier holding out his mess tin: 'You spineless coward – what type of men are you – trouser shitters – you should be ashamed – have somebody kick your arse – and no soup!' However funny it may have seemed at the time, this cannonade of abuse was not without its serious side and in a way we really were put to shame by this woman for not having done better to hold the enemy. I would have believed her capable of fighting in the front line, ready to die there.

The penultimate day of the retreat was either 31 January or the following day when we reached the Narva River before dusk. We saw a coffee house and decided to have something to warm up. So what could go wrong? We had our written orders. Unwashed and unshaved for days and carrying all our weapons we entered a very large room with nice subdued lighting, white table cloths, more soldiers than civilians being present – but the soldiers were neat and tidy, uniforms pressed – the *Etappe*. Being somewhat intimidated by the cultural atmosphere we were looking around for a discreet table when some field gendarmes espied us and demanded our papers. Confidently, Unteroffizier Dreihsen produced our orders. The field gendarme cast an eye over them fleetingly, then stuffed them into his pocket. 'This movement order is invalid. It has been countermanded. Come with me.' To Unteroffizier Dreihsen's objection he responded, 'I'm sorry, the order of the army corps commander, General von Brasse,[1] overrides all others.' Nothing could be clearer. Like condemned convicts we made our way to a collection centre escorted by the field gendarmes. The centre was a massive building with tiled floor and iron bars at each window including the toilets. Therefore escape was out of the question. We were told by other infantrymen that those men rounded up by the *Heldenklau*[2] were transported by the quickest possible route to the Kingisepp front. It was exactly what we seven had sworn never to accept: to be merged into a strange 'fire brigade unit'.

It was about 1900 hrs when we were led out to be loaded aboard transports. Above the entrance of the building was a feeble lamp and close by it a truck with tarpaulin cover. Nearby stood two field gendarmes and in the background a general. Suddenly we heard him shout, 'Stay here! Halt! Stay here!' and then, pistol drawn, he gave chase to several soldiers who had taken to their heels into the darkness. Mindful of their duty the two gendarmes followed the general. Now we seven stood all alone one behind the other in the doorway facing the truck, Dreihsen leading. After three seconds of indecision Dreihsen bolted into the gloom and we followed him down a back alley into the blacked-out streets of the town. We heard heavy boots approaching and hid as best we could in the porch of a house, listening anxiously. Dreihsen said softly, 'You all know what this is, don't you? It's desertion. If they catch us we will hang.' We hadn't thought of that. The sound of the boots grew fainter and now we discussed the situation. We knew that all the streets in and out of Narva had been sealed by the field gendarmes and we had no chance of getting through that way. Our alternative was to get to the outskirts and head across country to the road along the river bank from where we could make for Jõhvi. The purpose of our desertion was not to desert, but to obey orders to make for our regiment at Jõhvi. We reached the outskirts, passed the town's rubbish dump, and saw open snow-covered country ahead, its cow pastures enclosed by barbed-wire fencing. Beyond, the horizon was lit up. We could tell by the North Star which way was west, and the headlamps of the vehicles using the highway were bright enough for us to orient ourselves even at this distance.

There was only a light frost. The snow was knee-deep but we did not let that hold us back, continuing to trudge wearily past barbed-wire fencing and across small streams. At last we came to a column of trucks on the road. A driver we approached agreed that we could conceal ourselves under the tarpaulins covering the load in the rear of his vehicle. Then the truck set off slowly for Jõhvi, a couple of hours' drive.

'Haaalt! To which unit do you belong? Do you have any stragglers in your vehicle?' the field gendarme demanded. My heart beat as fast as it had during the T-34 attack. 'No.' was the driver's decisive answer. The beam of a pocket torch wandered over the load, lingered for a second over my hiding place and was then turned off. '*Weiterfahren!*' We had made it. We found our regiment and the signals platoon and were given two to three days to freshen up in Estonian dwellings, received a fresh issue of equipment and were then sent to the new front, the Panther Line between Narva and Lake Peipus.

Chapter 11 Notes

1. No 'General von Brasse' ever existed. *Trans.*
2. *Heldenklau* was a derogatory term for field gendarmes roughly translated as 'Hero-snatchers'. *Trans.*

CHAPTER 12

On the Narva Front

AT THE CONCLUSION OF THE RETREAT from Leningrad, the remnants of our division, already showing clear signs of disintegration, had to be re-assembled, re-organised, re-armed and the psychological will to fight on had to be restored to such an extent that an operation promising success against the advancing Russians would be possible. The losses in personnel had been made good partially by an infantry regiment sent out from Germany and the remnants of 9th Luftwaffe Division. But tested, veteran troops are not replaceable. All the same, the Russians were eventually repelled. That this was possible was, in my opinion, almost exclusively an achievement of the army leadership, of well-functioning supply and above all the composure and vision of the officer corps within the regiments. The company commanders and their platoon leaders radiated calm and composure. It was especially important that this moral strength should be regenerated after the weeks of disorganised retreat, and it was certainly decisive for the defensive successes which were to follow.

Before 61st Division was capable of operations again, the Russians succeeded in putting men across the frozen Narva and set up a not insignificant bridgehead in the area of Krivasoo. It was now of the greatest importance that this bridgehead should be destroyed. Bitter fighting raged, the brunt of it being borne by 162nd Grenadier Regiment. Any description by me would not do justice to the self-sacrificial involvement of these men, besides which I know few of the details.

As previously at Lake Ladoga and on the Volkhov, we found ourselves once again in swampy territory. The reorganised

Two assault boats in choppy seas heading for the Baltic island of Moon.

regiment under Oberst Müller-Melahn defended courageously but could not prevent a major breakthrough, but then under his leadership the Russians were forced back – for which he received the Knight's Cross. At centre stage here was Valvara station

on the Narva–Reval railway line where fighting resulted in the enemy force being wiped out. The obstacle for them was our MG 42 nests, and Russian bodies lay on the field in their hundreds. To the forefront were East Prussian troops with their own brand of steadfastness, assisted by many Rhinelanders, Westphalians, a handful of Saxons, Austrians and Sudeten Germans. East Prussia seemed to have been bled so dry that its regiments could no longer be reinforced by local recruits, the companies being at best only one-third East Prussian.

The front stabilised and now we began to think we could totally destroy the Russian bridgehead, which had been split into a western and an eastern part. Our regiment was selected for a leading role because we had experience of the type of terrain. I was present for the first two days of this operation, on 19 and 20 April 1944.

'I Die For Greater Germany'

I have chosen this cry from the lips of a dying man as a chapter sub-heading because there cannot have been many mortally wounded men who in their death throes willingly acknowledged sacrificing their lives for Greater Germany. The purpose of our impending attack was to clear out the Russian bridgehead and so extend our front the whole length of the banks of the Narva. What made the undertaking so difficult were the bottomless swamps. The winter of 1943 had been relatively mild and by mid-April the swamps had all thawed.

At 0435 hrs on 19 April 1944, at the edge of the swampy region south of Auvere, I shouldered my radio equipment and followed 2nd Battalion, 151st Grenadier Regiment. All I knew was that a panzer group would be coming from the west, that we would meet it on some road or other and by so doing successfully complete the operation. The morning had already dawned grey when we reached the starting point and formed into single file to trudge along a marshy beaten track. To its left and right stood dispersed, crippled pines, shrubby beeches, carefully tended willows and alders, dried clusters of grass, also reeds, swamp rushes and water lilies – just a portion of the swamp flora native to the region which would come to life in May.

Our artillery barrage petered out having probably had the desired effect, though also alerting the Russians that something was up. Hauptmann Krieg led our battalion from the front, holding a new German quick-fire assault rifle in his right hand. It was seen occasionally in the possession of leaders of companies.

Russian defensive fire came first from rifles then mortars. Their artillery joined in later. There was no cover, for only seldom could a spot be found dry enough in which to lie flat. Everywhere swamp and mud. Our task was to advance, difficult against a concealed enemy. Suddenly I sank to the waist in mud, into a shell crater which had filled with slime. There were many of them. I heaved myself up and waded forward in knee-high gravy. Fountains of mud rose up all around from the shelling. This was an advantage of the swamp: the splinter effect was less, the shells pretty much fizzling out on impact. Wounded men were calling for medical orderlies; others who couldn't go on sank down in the mud and either suffocated or drowned.

We reached a position evacuated by the enemy. These were field bunkers in which one literally had to stand up to stare – briefly. The most important thing in German bunker design was that they should be easy to enter and have space in which to stand up inside. The Russian bunker aimed for maximum

The fine St Catherine's church on the island of Moon, September 1941.

safety. They were built about two metres high above ground level. From the exterior one could see only very narrow shooting or viewing slits. The entrances were no more than 70 centimetres high and access was by crawling. The bunkers themselves had five or more tiers of tree trunks with earth layers between for the roof whereas only two tiers was generally the case with ours. Because of the massive thickness of the roof, there was only room inside the bunker to sit. In my opinion a Russian bunker of this kind would withstand a direct hit by a 105-mm shell. A Russian bunker complex would have log paths 60 to 70 centimetres wide, but the ones we inspected had been much damaged by shelling and were blanketed with mud.

The enemy defensive fire intensified and our attack came to a standstill. Initially we sought cover behind stacks of empty ammunition boxes, though these were in fact useless against even a rifle bullet. The enemy were to the south of us on the far side of a valley that presumably would have a brook or small river flowing through it. To satisfy my curiosity I took a chance and raised my head for a quick look at the other side of the valley. The Russians were at about the same height as ourselves and we could see their reinforcements creeping up through the undergrowth. Hauptmann Krieg now stood upright firing long bursts from his new weapon into the creeping Russians. It was a practical weapon and light to handle: it made the old '98 carbine obsolete. I didn't need to carry mine any longer; the radio troop leader was allowed to make do with a .38 pistol.

The landing stage from where men of 151st Infantry Regiment embarked into assault boats for the conquest of Moon.

It should really have been obvious to an experienced company commander that this fearless standing-and-firing attitude could simply not go on for long. Shortly afterwards I saw him going to the rear with an emergency dressing on his arm. This was the last operation in the war for this valiant infantry officer. Presumably he finished his career with the Wound Badge in Gold, having collected the Silver version at Lake Ladoga. It was a pity: one fewer of the old guard, to whom one looked up and who had a sense of humour. So, without Hauptmann Krieg we faced an enemy growing in numbers. More frequently we found ourselves sinking down to waist level in the mire.

As our misery worsened the heavens were suddenly filled with the sound of a group of twenty-seven Stukas forming up ready to attack. Sirens of Jericho howling, like enormous hornets they tipped over their wings and dived on the Russian readiness positions opposite. One machine after another plunged towards the target, released its bomb load, pulled out close to the ground and with motor howling regained altitude. Some of their bombs opened craters in the swamps. Approaching again from a wide curve at the right height they repeated the performance as before, dropped their bombs and, as suddenly as they had appeared, disappeared from the skies once again.

Our struggle against the Russians, and more so the swamps, continued. Despite the Stukas our advance bogged down: the ground conditions suppressed every effort. The promised panzer attack never materialised for the same reason. Nobody who was there and survived this Führer's birthday of 1944 will ever forget it. Unteroffizier Crimerius of 2nd Battalion signals staff passed me carrying his radio apparatus, collapsed in exhaustion on a large case, his steel helmet at an angle like a drunken *Uhlan* [lancer]: all he wanted to do was take a breather. It was our final meeting before he found his last rest.

As evening fell, Unteroffizier von Ulardt arrived with his telephone troop to lay a line. The men of the infantry companies had to remain outside all night with no relief, trembling in their filthy wet uniforms, damp and cold penetrating to their bones. They had to come to terms with adversity and get through it. I was lucky and had to return to regimental HQ. The two-man Morse section was allotted quarters in an Estonian farmhouse where we could dry our clothes and get warm before a stove.

Ulardt's telephone squad had come under mortar fire and barricaded themselves behind the empty ammunition boxes. A mortar bomb hit and blew the boxes apart. Georg Lehr, a member of this squad, cried out: 'I am wounded – I am dying. I die for Greater Germany. I die for Greater Germany . . .' With these last words his voice weakened. Wolfgang knelt at his side and tried to dress the wounds but saw at once that it was hopeless. Holding up the dying man's head he put his field flask filled with coffee to the man's lips and urged him not to give up. Obergefreiter Lehr could no longer understand. Weakness overcame him, and he closed his eyes for ever. His last thoughts were for Germany, for which he had given his life – Greater Germany as he called it. The *Obergefreiter* with the yellow silk scarf around his neck was a cheerful man and the only soldier I ever knew who died with the word 'Germany' on his lips. He was a *Volksdeutscher* [ethnic German] from Poland.

After two or three days they withdrew our shrivelled companies from the front. The attack had failed. Not until the warmer months would the entire west bank of the Narva be back in German hands. Our military cemetery at Toila had grown larger by many graves. At the end of May 1944 the regiment moved to a quiet position near the 'children's home'. This was a building formerly used for that purpose, standing in its own grounds, but was for us simply a place where we could rest and recuperate. At this time in Toila there was even a concert party with a troupe of six. The four girls of the ensemble used to sun themselves by day in a quiet corner of the regimental command post. There being no competition, they apparently enjoyed being the centre of attention.

There is nothing of value to report about the subsequent weeks. I was made an instructor, and given the task of training young soldiers of the infantry company on the new model field telephone. This equipment was designed to enable a better connection between the platoons and company command posts. I looked for a quiet spot on the Baltic coast for our training exercises. Behind a steep embankment we enjoyed warm sunshine, the smell of the earth and coastal grasses, and a warm breeze. Way below us on the sands stood the tall chimney and buildings of an abandoned cellulose factory. The Baltic sea was deserted, no ships, no fishing vessels, nothing. The sea was mostly calm apart from a slight swell.

CHAPTER 13

Back into Latvia

IN THE SECOND HALF OF JUNE 1944 a new Soviet offensive achieved a major breakthrough against Army Group Centre in the area of Minsk. The heavily hit divisions of Sixteenth Army attempted to set up a new defensive line at the Düna. Although our division, part of Eighteenth Army, was only a skeleton formation, we had to play the fire brigade role again. From Jõhvi we were taken by train to Dünaburg in south-east Latvia. Russian aircraft circled above as we unloaded, but we suffered no losses. After that we found the situation to be lively and confused because mostly, or very often, we had no idea of where the front line was, and where the rear. Therefore it so happened that an American jeep with Russian officers came driving up to us quite unsuspectingly on the Birsen road: our regimental adjutant, I think it was Oberleutnant Koschorrek, had a similar misfortune riding his staff motorcycle. As for us radio operators, as a result of this uncertainty the need arose to take down Morse messages using only one earpiece of the headphones, the other ear being free to keep a sharp listening watch for what was going on outside, since it seemed relatively easy to be 'nabbed'. The era of unconditional trust in our infantry companies, namely that where they stood no Russian could pass, was long gone, the sectors of the front were simply too huge and could only be monitored from strongpoints along their length.

The summer months of 1944 also saw the beginning of streams which grew ever greater the nearer they came to the borders of the Reich, until finally like an avalanche they spread over the whole area east of the Oder and Neisse: the streams of refugees. *Volksdeutscher* from the Polish regions and Baltic peoples set it in

Generalmajor Gottfried Weber seen wearing his Knight's Cross with Oakleaves.

motion. They knew from experience what they could expect when the Russians returned. Many therefore preferred an uncertain future with the Germans troops to transportation, rape or murder under the Red Army.

For me, my introduction to the fighting in Courland was at Birsen. Here we were welcomed by a hail of Stalin-organ rockets which landed in the centre of our readiness position on the outskirts of town. Oberfeldwebel Hofer and I emerged from a trench to find that the leafy roof over our heads had been swept away by the blasts leaving only mutilated bare branches. A splinter hit the lid of a cooking pot, but nobody was hurt. Almost at once we began to receive increasing supplies of heavy weapons. Where they came from was a mystery. Tiger and versatile Panther tanks, self-propelled assault guns and howitzers, 2-cm flak guns for ground combat and of course artillery and rocket-launcher brigades. Also present was Luftwaffe Oberst Rudel with his anti-tank squadron of Stukas, which engaged Soviet tanks from the air, watched by friend and foe. When one remembers that the Stalin tanks had a 12.2-cm cannon, the size of the debt we owed to Oberst Rudel and his pilots for the number of enemy tanks they destroyed will be understood. Rudel was revered by the simple soldier in the trenches. Today no German is supposed to think in that way; while other nations esteem and honour their heroes even when the cause was evil, Germany's heroes must all be deprecated for the same patriotic sentiments.

These weapons reinforced the fighting spirit of our troops. As an example of what I mean I would like to provide the following experience: in very difficult situations involving the regiment, the pioneer platoon with its seventy or so men was often the last available reserve. At Birsen I was present at an action to seal a stretch of our front line. The pioneer platoon had dug in on a slope at the edge of a field. The slope was overgrown with bushes. There was an excellent field of fire. Our radio point was by a heavy machine-gun nest manned by three young East Prussians, former

Heinz Schimanski, Fritz Krebs and the author, Erhard Steiniger, received the radio message at 0550 hrs on 14 September 1941 reporting the arrival of 1st Battalion, 151st Infantry Regiment, off the village of Kuivastu on the island of Moon and in desperate trouble.

farm workers. In expectation of action, No. 1 gunner was calmly eating a lard sandwich. The Russian infantry were advancing across open ground towards us in a frontal assault They were in several ranks. 'When are you going to open fire?' I asked him.

'Not yet, let them come,' he said with a confident grin, though without ever taking his eyes off them for a moment. Then after a last mouthful he said, 'Now they're close enough,' turned the machine gun to rake the enemy troops, and opened fire, his No. 2 lying close by, feeding him the belt. He kept firing short bursts into the Russians, none of whom got closer than thirty metres, at which point death would come to meet them. Thus the attack was warded off. Steadfast in obedience to their orders, in those months of retreat our comrades-in-arms and our weapons secured such defensive victories against considerable odds.

The overall German situation made me feel uncomfortable. It was not only the continuing success of the Normandy landings since 6 June but that there was apparently no way out of the war except unconditional surrender. No matter where he might stand in the political spectrum, no German would find that solution desirable. Then came the attempt to assassinate Hitler on 20 July. What did most Wehrmacht men think of that? On reflection, it was a mixture of hope and revulsion that we felt. Hope, because there were apparently people in the officer corps prepared to save what could be saved from the lost war. This could only be done without Hitler, therefore the assassination attempt. On the other hand revulsion because such an attitude had to be

Repair work proceeding on the four-kilometre-long Ösel causeway damaged in places by the Russians and captured by 7th Company, 151st Infantry Regiment.

classified as high treason and a rejection of the personal oath of loyalty. Loyalty and reliability, particularly in crisis situations, had always been the hallmark of the Prussian officer.

On 9 August 1944, at the time the Russian infantry launched their frontal attack on the machine-gun nest as mentioned above, I wrote a field letter to my intended: 'Things are going better for me at the moment. We are on the Latvian–Lithuanian border near Birsen and have now finally occupied a position which we hope to develop as we wish. The *Tross* still have my blankets and so I cover myself with straw in a hole in the ground. It has been days since I last heard a Wehrmacht Bulletin. It is being rumoured that Tilsit is to be evacuated. That cannot be! If we no longer have the strength to repel the enemy, then every sacrifice made will be in vain. The leadership knows that and so I do not believe it.'

We were called upon to help out again. The front had been forced back from Estonia. Latvian and Estonian units formed to defend their countries were not reliable; the soldiers preferred to abandon the front in favour of their farms and towns. Who could blame them? They wanted to save their skins insofar as that was still possible under the circumstances. Therefore the advancing Russians had to be stopped on the Latvian–Estonian frontier.

Our regimental signals platoon had been motorised for greater mobility. We had been given a box-type van and a driver with very modest skills. Changing our position one night, two of us sat between our signals equipment, rocking back and forth in the back of the van within a convoy of vehicles heading for a new defensive line at Segewold. Our driver had only to follow the vehicle ahead, which he could see with slit headlamps, but ran our box van down a four-metre slope and overturned it. We had no time to react, men and equipment were flung together and my nose was hit by the edge of the steel housing of my 44-pound radio pack. Dazed and bleeding, I was given an emergency dressing and taken next day to a field hospital where I was diagnosed with a broken nose and haemorrhage in the eye sockets. This gave my face the appearance of a barn owl. These were injuries and not wounds and so did not classify me for the Wound Badge in Silver.

I was sent to the *Tross* as unfit for duty, and from there was a spectator to the raging close-combat in the thick woodlands, and the accompanying panzer battle. Werner Hafenbier lost his No. 2 radioman Kurt Fiedler from Dresden, shot through the head.

Hafenbier's description of this battle was enough to convince me not to regret having missed out on it.

The name of General Schörner belongs in these memories of Courland. Through his drastic actions to obtain men for the front, he soon became the bogeyman of the *Tross*. He would appear unannounced amidst the rear units and, using some personal yardstick and his own judgement, comb through them with a view to increasing the trench strengths of the infantry companies. What were urgently needed were close-combat troops able to tackle a tank with a Panzerfaust or limpet mine: whether these very often elderly *Tross* men were suitable for the role is another question. Soon the craziest tales were circulating about Schörner. Depending on his mood he would have his driver stop on the road and either demote or promote someone there and then. Despite his choleric outbursts, however, which often manifested on his visits to troop units, he was a very successful commander and the stabilising of the Courland front was in many respects his doing.

Meanwhile Russian tanks had reached the Baltic at Tuckum. Weak German counter-attacks resulted in high losses. The Russians broke through on a wide front at Schaulen from where they reached Tilsit and Memel on 9 November 1944 cutting off Army Group North from East Prussia. German forces relinquished Riga on 11 November and on Hitler's orders Sixteenth Army and Eighteenth Army, of which my regiment usually formed part, withdrew into the Courland peninsula. The bastion stood firm, serving no particular purpose but resisted yielding the peninsula until the capitulation.

Wainoden

Our detached regiment had been stopped at Wainoden on 8 October and sent in battle order southwards.

From a side road, a truck came racing towards us, full of Luftwaffe signals girls, some with hair flying, fear and horror in their faces. They had come from the Wainoden airfield, which had

On foot, with horse and cart, and on bicycles, 151st Infantry Regiment advancing to Kärdla, main settlement on the island of Dagö. To the right, Leutnant Heckler.

just been abandoned by one of our fighter squadrons before the Russian attack spearhead arrived. We realised that contact with the enemy could not now be far off; they were probing, infiltrating, finding gaps everywhere, and this in a densely forested area.

Our first command post was set up in a sanatorium, still peaceful. We were invited into a music room where a quartet made

up of patients played baroque music for us. The two young women and two young men put great effort into it, and we were not sparing with our applause. Towards evening we left the sanatorium silently to occupy a more suitable defensive line. We had just dug in when, at 2200 hrs, we saw four young Latvian girls, without shoes, wearing only socks, totally distressed and exhausted, being led towards our rearward services. We discovered that, after we pulled out, the Russians took over the sanatorium where they raped the nurses, female patients and kitchen staff. These four had seized the opportunity provided by the horror and confusion of the scene to reach the German lines across swampy woodland.

From this point on, we began to see more and more Estonian and Latvian refugees carrying all their belongings in backpacks. They were all heading for Libau on the Courland peninsula, the only seaport still in German hands. Wolfgang said, 'Just imagine our families having to escape like that.' We kept our thoughts to ourselves. There was no more time for sombre reflection. From the following day we were forced to keep the Russians at bay without heavy weapons, our own artillery still being on its way. If at all possible we avoided close combat on account of being so heavily outnumbered as to be easily overrun; an elastic policy was more expedient. Our rocket-launcher teams helped us tremendously.

It was a week of bitter fighting at Wainoden. In a field-post letter of 15 October 1944 I wrote to my unofficial fiancée: 'Today, a Sunday, I was relieved for a couple of days and was able to cleanse

The onset of winter, northern Russia, 1941. The photo shows the Hermannsfeste fortress (left), established by the Teutonic Knights in 1380 on the western bank of the River Narva, and the Ivangorod fort on the eastern bank. The author was billeted in the Hermannsfeste at Narva for a few days during the advance to Tikhvin.

The village of Pertetshno on the River Volkhov, snowed in during the winter of 1941. It was the scene of heavy fighting after the Wehrmacht withdrew from Tikhvin in December 1941.

myself of a whole week's filth. I felt new-born. They were difficult days we had to endure. Two days ago Ivan almost nabbed me. The Russians had broken through again and were facing the battalion command post positioned at most only 300 to 500 metres behind our main front line. When the commanding officer shouted,

"Telegraphists, into the woods, quickly!" we needed no second bidding, though it meant crossing an open field with our heavy equipment on our backs. It was a miracle that we were not hit in this hellfire. So you see, my good luck has not deserted me, though one of our telephone linesmen, Fritz Krebs, was shot in the head leaving his hole in the ground.

'Today I found out something of the overall situation. The enemy is already north of Tilsit and Memel, sad but true. This means that we are practically encircled and I have no means of knowing if the field post can get through to you. The most difficult times of all will now probably confront you personally. You and your parents will have to leave your dear homeland. It is to be despaired! I have heard nothing from my own home for three weeks. Since the events in Romania I have received no news from my brother Franz. I think he is listed as missing. It's all the same to me. I am just begging you to flee so as to avoid falling into the hands of the Russians. I shall not write anything more on the subject except to say that they do what they like to women and girls. If Fate permits us to meet again then I shall be able to tell you what I know. And you will also have many terrible things to tell. It is all so sad. All one can say is, "Poor Germany. You have fought like lions and must bleed to death because you have the whole world as your enemy."'

After this letter I was not involved in any further fighting in Courland. Our companies there were practically wiped out and the remnants of the regiment retired to be disbanded and

Members of 2nd Battalion, 151st Infantry Regiment, on New Year's Eve, 1941. This flash photo, taken with the help of powder from two bullets, shows from left to right, rear row: Feldwebel Mack, Heinz

Schimanski, Hans Weber, the author Erhard Steiniger, Hans Gudde and (first name unknown) Crimerius. At the front (holding bottle) Feldwebel Heinrich, Otto Grau, unknown, and Karlheinz Crusius.

then be re-formed as 2nd Battalion, 162nd Grenadier Regiment. After a few quiet days, at the end of October we were taken to Libau where two 6,000-ton freighters were waiting for us in the port. Before we could board the Russians bombed them from a great altitude: a neighbouring house was hit and collapsed. I got out covered in dust and filth and a few splinters of glass. In my field post letter of 9 November I wrote: 'Now a brief mention of my experiences. After we had been given a drubbing in the heavy fighting south-east of Libau, after several days' rest we proceeded to the port to embark. Everything went off quietly except for two bombing raids. I was lucky: in the first, the bombs dropped on a neighbouring house, and in the second the bombs fell in the water straddling the ship. The voyage in a 6,000-ton steamer passed without incident. I wasn't even seasick. From Gotenhafen we went by train to Königsberg. There was a short stop at Elbing, and on the other platform was a passenger train with evacuated Tilsiters. Our platoon commander called out for you, and I tried to find you, but in vain. This was on 30 October, when you were already at Braunsberg. We were unloaded at Insterburg and marched to south-east of Gumbinnen where we were placed in a slit trench on the front line with our radio equipment. Over the last two nights we two telegraphists enlarged the hole so that we can at least turn round, and we also put a layer of beams overhead. We have both got heavy colds. Today is the sixth we have spent in this hole without any chance to warm up.'

Christmas 1941 at 162nd Grenadier Regiment. Hauptmann Wilhelm Kubel and to his right (with rings on lower sleeve) Hauptfeldwebel (Regimental Sergeant-Major) Lindenblatt. Hauptmann Kubel received the award of the Knight's Cross on 30 September 1944.

Several lines later in this four-page letter I wrote: 'I had to interrupt writing this letter to help carry away two wounded, one being the company commander. Unfortunately our assistance was of no avail: they both died on the stretcher. One had been

Spring 1942: the thaw caused the Volkhov to burst its banks. The water reached the command post of 2nd Battalion, 151st Infantry Regiment, and flooded these graves.

shot in the head, the other received an explosive bullet through the thigh and bled to death. It shows once more the policy of the Russian High Command. We have already come to terms with it.'

This was my last direct involvement in the fighting on any front. On 11 November 1944, in a reshuffle, my previous field post number was restored and we were once again the regimental signals platoon; Major Krüger was made commanding officer of 151st Grenadier Regiment. Leutnant Reuter, formerly signals staff leader of 2nd Battalion, 151st Infantry Regiment, became adjutant.

Before going on with my story, I would like to set down my impressions regarding our defensive situation. In East Prussia there were two things which caught my attention:

(1) *The position, behind our foremost lines,* was outstandingly constructed. It even had communication trenches with roofs, something we had never seen before in the entire war.

(2) *The yawning gaps in the most forward lines.* I am not exaggerating when I say that I always had the eerie impression, on these flat, wide pasturelands south-east of Gumbinnen, that we telegraphists were alone. We could see a single sentry to the right and left about 200 metres off, and nothing else. The 'reserves', who were to render the remnants of the regiment capable of holding off the Red Army, were most elderly men, amongst them many from the Austrian and Bavarian Alps who had left their mountain farms and alpine pastures for the first time in their lives and were trusting in prayer to stay alive. When Russian scouting parties approached, they crouched in their holes praying instead of shooting and throwing hand-grenades – or some at least! These were really the very last reserves being sent like lambs to the slaughter. In my opinion it can only have been done to give the East Prussian population the chance to get out. The expectation that the East Prussian divisions would cling to their homeland could not be fulfilled for they practically no longer existed. In reality these 'divisions' were just fragments to be pushed around a map table at Führer-HQ in the pretence that they were complete divisions. We were at our end.

Our regimental command post was at Altkrug near Gumbinnen where I was made signals-platoon clerk. My duties involved drawing up new code tables and encryption files. Since there was nothing else to do I also manned the small drop-flap telephone exchange. What I got to overhear filled me with horror. Almost daily, reconnaissance reported columns of Russian trucks coming up, sometimes 120 trucks, then 80 and then 160 again: always heading west. They were bringing up ammunition for their artillery to bury us. We had to look on helplessly as the Russians worked in great numbers all day, and then in the evenings continued under electrical lighting. In order to fire even nuisance

Near the command post of 151st Infantry Regiment at Dmitrovka in the spring of 1942; a period of mud always followed the thaw. Here a horse makes better progress than an engine of many horse-power.

rounds at them, our artillery had to ask the permission of corps to shoot, and would then be permitted to fire five or seven rounds, only enough to get the range to the target. How lucky we were that the Russians did not begin their major offensive – our last battle – there and then.

My final Christmas with the Wehrmacht came. I was sharing a small house on a settlement with Oberfeldwebel Hofer, Wolfgang and a fourth man. It required a lot of cleaning, even the portraits and furniture had to be dusted, chairs washed and floors scrubbed. The official celebrations began about eight in the evening with poems and Christmas stories, then we listened to Dr Goebbels's speech before celebrating with the rest. I brewed up a liqueur which we were enjoying when my unofficial fiancée rang me. We met on Boxing Day for six hours at Insterburg: our adjutant, Leutnant Reuter, told me to go there and fetch signals equipment. It has a special memory for both of us, the embodiment of a happy reunion and a sad farewell for years.

On 11 January 1945 Oberfeldwebel Hofer surprised me by saying, 'Make sure you've got the encryption files ready. Then you can go to the *Tross* tomorrow and start your leave on the 13th.' He only needed to tell me once. I went to the *Tross* and had my leave pass in my pocket on the night of the 12th. Next morning I went to Insterburg and prepared to leave early next day for home. At 0700 hrs on 13 January we came under sustained Stalin-organ fire as a prelude to the major offensive – an incessant, constant distant drumming from hundreds of launchers along the whole front. Window panes rattled. Although it was expected, we were all affected by it. Within the hour the report came that Russian tanks were pushing towards us from Ebenrode. The *Tross* now began to load up in a frenzy. I watched it woebegone, for I saw my leave evaporating:

I was still short of the signature of a medical officer on my leave pass to the effect that I was free of any infectious disease or vermin, but the doctors had all left already for the main dressing stations.

At Headquarters Company the staff veterinary officer Dr Krämer listened to my problem. 'What, that's all you need? Well, we can't have you losing your leave just for that. Do you swear you have no infectious disease or lice?' I said no and he held out his hand. 'Give me the pass. I'm also a doctor!' and signed it. 'So, don't let yourself be snared on the way and get home safely!' I detected a certain wistfulness in his last words. I went to Insterburg and set off. I am still so grateful to that man today for his signature, for it set the course for my future survival. Everything then went without a hitch. At Korschen my leave pass was studied very carefully before I was allowed to continue. The feared ban on leave-taking came into effect on 15 January, by when I was already home. I arrived during an air-raid warning. The synthetic oil plant at Brüx, where benzine was produced from brown coal, was often the target of bombing raids, and my home village was only twenty kilometres from there.

Morale in the Sudetenland was poor although here and there people still nursed a kind of magical belief in the Führer. 'The V-Weapons are up to V-10. He is bound to have something with which he can win this war.' But the majority had only one question: 'What will become of us if we lose?' The fear of the fanatical Czechs was on the rise, as it had been at the time of the Sudeten crisis. The *Bürgermeister* made regular visits to individual Czech farmers in the district. He got his reinsurance at Jaroslav Soucek's, and while other Nazi Party functionaries were killed off, he escaped with his life.

On 4 February 1945 my leave ended and the hour came to depart. I left my parents' house by the back yard, went through the big garden behind the barn and headed for the station across the fields, lightly covered with snow. My parents had tears in their eyes, although I know they tried to avoid making my departure a

August 1942. The author and a local trading partner bartering bread for raspberries.

A heavy-machine-gun position in the Grusino bridgehead, which the Russians attempted to storm without success.

sad one. I asked them to stay indoors and not watch me leaving. I did not look back. Perhaps it was a farewell for ever, for all of us.

Once clear, I paused to look at the village where I was born and grew up, knowing that this German homeland would soon become a battlefield for its inhabitants. A last look over the roofs of the community of 2,000 souls, at the protruding red onion-dome of the church with its golden cross, and I knew that this would be my last farewell.

My unit no longer existed. My association with the regimental signals platoon of 151st Grenadier Regiment, 61st East Prussian

Infantry Division, terminated on 13 January 1945. The battle for East Prussia began that day, and during the following weeks the division went under. Shoulder to shoulder with other exhausted Wehrmacht units deployed in East Prussia it offered resistance until the last of its blood drained out with its back to the Baltic. On 10 April 1945 the remnants paraded for the last time before the Königsberg playhouse, and then marched off into captivity. In the six years of war, 61st Division sustained the following losses: 4,500 fallen, 3,000 missing, 21,000 wounded: a total of 28,500 officers and men. Not only sacrifices of lives are to be mourned but also the unimaginable physical and mental strain, deprivation and self-abnegation of all kinds which had to be endured and survived. For almost four and a half years I was a member of the regimental signals platoon of 151st Grenadier Regiment. I was spared the last bitter episode in the circle of my comrades-in-arms. I was forced to tread this path of humiliation and degradation later without them. I do not know which of them lost their lives in those last weeks; I included them all – living and dead – in my memory on Remembrance of Heroes Day.

In his history of 61st Infantry Division, Walther Hubatsch asked a question to which no satisfactory answer can yet be found, namely the sense of this sacrifice. He wrote: 'We, as those who experienced it, will not yet be able to answer this question. The historical effect of such sacrifice is liable not to become visible until much later. But it never remains without its consequences. It is just as valid today as in previous times that such an achievement as has been displayed here would not have been possible without those inner values lived during the six years of war and which for many were sealed with death: obedience, loyalty, discipline, comradeship, fulfilment of duty unto death, and setting aside one's own interests in devotion to the common cause. Are all these values to be buried with our dead?'

The main railway station at Dresden always marked for me the end of my leave. East Prussia was now no longer reachable, cut off. We returners from leave were collected at Dresden in the Hindenburg Barracks. Elegant, beautiful Dresden, the city of gardens and culture, provided in those days the picture of a city in grey, hopelessly swamped by tens of thousands of pitiable refugees. The majestic façades of its baroque houses stood in sharp contrast to the great horde of its new inhabitants.

We were confined to barracks. On 7 or 8 February there was an air-raid alarm. British reconnaissance aircraft circled above the city at great altitude, unopposed. What would they want here? Dresden did have a cigarette industry, but hardly worth the attention of Allied bombers, or so we thought. The same day a start was made on forming a march battalion [reinforcement unit]. These were mainly signals and *Tross* people, few infantry. Although no signals equipment was available, a signals group was formed to which I was attached. I noticed that the *Oberleutnant* selecting the signals group took only infantry-signals men. Those with the yellow braid of the signals branch were formed into an anti-tank troop.

Our train pulled out of Dresden on 9 February 1945 exactly four days before the sadistic massacre by the Royal Air Force and Americans. In the same way that the Holocaust will forever remain Germany's shame, the carpet bombing of German cities, and in particular the murderous attack on Dresden, will remain theirs. From the military point of view the city had absolutely no importance, only its cultural heritage. I knew Dresden before the war. I believed it was the most beautiful and cleanest German city.

Many a brave horse lost its life in the mud. Here horses from the telephony waggon are being used to pull a supply cart: one of the pair has collapsed exhausted in the mud and will be shot.

We were unloaded at Striegau in Silesia. The barracks here had been evacuated and we were now apparently the only force available to delay the enemy. First we had to be armed. The empty barracks were scoured for weapons and ammunition. We came up with a couple of Panzerfaust infantry anti-tank rockets but not one artillery piece. The march battalion was placed in and around the town at appropriate locations. The Kommandantur called for an NCO and three men of the signals group to relieve and take over the Striegau telephone exchange. I volunteered, incidentally the first time I ever volunteered for anything in the Wehrmacht. The take-over process meant ignoring all the bustle and clatter and having a look at commercial telephone technology. It was the first time we had ever seen anything like it. We did not have the foggiest idea what to make of the circuits and thousands of wires. It was quite hopeless and finally we were satisfied just to be able to contact the Kommandantur. That was definitely important!

August 1942. Members of the signals platoon, 151st Infantry, on the way to the Leningrad front. Rear row left to right, Tolksdorf, Feldwebel Hofer, Arnold Mathäus, Fritz Krebs, Wolfgang von Ulardt, Hans Greiner, Heinz Schimanski, Gustav Wachnowski, Alfred Janz; seated, Bubi Büchs, Werner Quellmalz, the author, Viktor Presch.

I noticed quite soon that our NCO was single-minded in his intention to survive the war. 'We must be careful not to overlook connections to the rear,' he said, 'and if the Russians come, we shall head for the Riesengebirge mountains and find a hayshed

there to sit it out.' That was our guiding light and we all accepted it. I wanted to survive too, not only to see what 'peace' looked like, but simply to go on living. On 11 February the managing director of the telephone exchange took his leave of us with two bottles of wine. From now on we eavesdropped every report made to and from the Kommandantur. Once it was news that sixty Russian tanks were heading for Striegau, then again that Russian infantry were approaching on foot. To take on the armoured force we did not have a single anti-tank gun, only the two Panzerfaust rockets.

At eight on the morning of 12 February I was reminded of the Volkhov front in its quietest moments when I heard a small amount of rifle fire and the occasional crack of a tank gun. Looking down on the street from the first floor I was horrified to see barely a hundred metres away two Russian tanks in line ahead with supporting infantry. Now we had to act fast. With a Panzerfaust on my shoulder, my new companions and I hurried down to the street behind the telephone exchange. I could probably have taken out the first tank without a problem if only . . . yes, if only I had known how to fire the Panzerfaust. I fiddled with it, tried this and that, and time ran out. The failure to train us signals people on that kind of weapon had taken its revenge and, unarmed, I was spared having to undergo the final test of courage.

Our NCO set off at once at the double for the western outskirts of town and we followed his lead. Once clear of Striegau – not very heroically – we continued in sunny winter weather heading cross-country for the Riesengebirge. The wind drove powder snow into our faces and howled past our ears. On the arterial road ahead we perceived a convoy of vehicles and a long stream of refugees; we made our way through them and continued towards the mountains. After having left this road some distance behind us we heard a call coming from afar. 'Don't turn round, keep going!' the NCO said. After a while another voice chimed in, 'We have to stop, there's an officer coming up behind us!' We had no choice but to halt. Now we would never reach the Riesengebirge. It was a *Hauptmann*, the *Kommandant* of Freiburg driving a Volkswagen amphibious car. 'Get in!'

I perched on a mudguard and we were driven between panzers on either side of the road moving up in battle order. At the entrance to the town of Freiburg stood a figure we recognised instantly. General Schörner was leading the counter-attack personally. Depending on how things were presented to him at this point we four might be hanging by the neck from nearby trees within a few minutes, I thought. The *Hauptmann* made his report to the *Generaloberst*, who moved his head in our direction and asked, 'Where have these birds of passage come from?' I could not hear the *Hauptmann*'s answer since he was standing with his back to us. Then Schörner said quite distinctly, 'And make sure they actually get there.' He meant the Front Collection Centre at Freiburg, which was located on a mountainside in a large clinker-brick establishment, the National Socialist Welfare Training College.

As I have emphasised repeatedly, a soldier needs luck in war. Truly I always had that little spark of luck that one needs for survival; when it counted it never deserted me. The last batch of stragglers had left the college only two hours previously either to dig trenches or as reserves for 208th Division, but we had to stay. General Schörner's counter-attack halted the Russian advance. The situation stabilised, and we were now added to the fifty-man reserve in the training college.

CHAPTER 14

I Become a Medical Orderly

I REPORTED SICK AT ONCE with laryngitis. Those of us on the sick list were assured that a doctor visited every day, and a few days later he arrived. The door of the first-floor surgery opened and a slender *Unterarzt* – a medical NCO of warrant officer rank in the *Gebirgsjäger*, of medium height, rosy cheeks and dimples – emerged with a smile. He addressed the illustrious company of sufferers: 'Which of you know orthography?' Apparently nobody, and so when he asked again I raised my hand. 'Please come in!' I had to draw up two dockets bearing the headings 'Certificate of Unfitness for Duty in the Field' and 'Only Suitable for Indoor Service' which he dictated to me, and then he signed them. This worked quite well, and when the last patient had left the surgery he asked me, 'And you. Are you also sick?' And so I came by my 'Certificate of Unfitness for Duty in the Field'.

'Tell you what, you'd be better off here in the surgery. You can sleep on the examination couch, which is better than lying on straw in the basement. It is your job to keep the room clean and in good order.' After some reflection he added, 'Can you type?' I nodded. 'Oh, that's excellent. We'll see how we get on together and perhaps then you'd like to remain with me.' Then he introduced himself formally: 'I am Dr August Czerwinski, and in civilian life I am a specialist in internal diseases.'

This was my first meeting with this fine man, impregnated with strong moral and religious principles. After the staff veterinary surgeon Dr Krämer, he was the second person who helped set the course decisively for my survival. I remain immensely indebted to him. He was never a soldier at heart, but a man thrust into uniform. He came from the University Clinic at Würzburg but was a native of Upper Silesia. Whenever he addressed me it was as '*Herr Steiniger*' and not '*Obergefreiter*'. 'You have to understand,' he told me once, 'this military form of address is pretty degrading. I don't leave the "*Herr*" off. You'll get used to it.' I also had the feeling that he had chosen me on account of the infantry assault badge on my left breast. He sought a certain moral support in my front experience. Without question he had guts and initiative, which in that era of our defeat was worth its weight in gold.

He appointed me as a clerk in the dispensary, or perhaps pharmacy clerk. This lasted a week and then Dr Czerwinski advised me that we had to set up an infirmary for the lightly wounded – General Schörner had issued an order that the lightly wounded were not to be sent behind the Freiburg–Schweidnitz Line for treatment. Our troops had recaptured Striegau, and Freiburg now lay fifteen kilometres behind the front. I had therefore become a soldier of the *Etappe*. Not only that, medicine began to draw me increasingly under its spell.

Upstairs on the first floor beside the examination room we requested and got three other rooms, a hall large enough for twelve metal-framed beds and a bathroom with running water and four tubs. I organised the other necessities, particularly cutlery and mess tins and to my surprise found everybody willing to help. Because I considered that the doctor ought to appear outwardly to be an officer I obtained an agreement with the clothing store NCO for officers' boots, a peaked cap, and riding breeches and tunic of the best quality material, made to measure by the company tailor. Now Unterarzt Dr Czerwinski could stand freshly clothed before the looking glass and smile, well pleased with himself from top to bottom, no doubt thinking of his wife and young daughter. The clothing store NCO suffered from sciatic nerve damage and could not walk far. He made everything possible based on my promise, which I kept, that he would be taken with us in the staff car when the time came to evacuate the institution.

Everyday routine and our new duties made their demands of us. We received as a medical orderly a Feldwebel Distelfink, by his insignia an officer cadet. He was a good-looking man in his later twenties, clever and educated. Two girls, his downfall, came daily to clean the rooms and wash the dishes, and the first ill men arrived, cases such as pneumonia, malaria, stomach illnesses and similar. On average our clinic would have eight or nine patients confined to bed each day. I was responsible for the office work, Feldwebel Distelfink was the doctor's assistant and senior charge nurse. After the doctor's rounds he would go over the individual cases and explain the treatment. I also had to perform the intra-muscular injections. 'It's quite simple; you draw an imaginary cross on the whole buttock and inject into the upper outer quadrant, because that is where the blood vessels are fewest. Naturally you have to clean the injection site beforehand with ether, pinch the skin between thumb and forefinger of the left hand and then jab confidently. Then a sticking plaster, finished.' The things a telegraphist was required to learn in the German Army.

On the evening of the *Feldwebel*'s birthday he celebrated in his room with the two cleaning girls – discreet lightning – while I tried to sleep on the examination couch in the adjacent room. This celebration lasted a week. One day Dr Czerwinski came up to me and announced, '*Herr* Steiniger, you will take over the whole shop immediately.'

'*Jawohl, Herr Unterarzt.*'

'You will have one of the patients to help you fetch and distribute the meals and so on. That should work nicely. Feldwebel Distelfink will be moving on.' With that I understood that I was to become the jack of all trades. My fear that the medical side of things would ask too much of me he brushed aside: 'I have been watching and have noticed that you have handled everything correctly until now. I have released Feldwebel Distelfink. Hauptmann Müller told me about the nightly celebrations up here.' The *Hauptmann* lived on the ground floor below us. Dr Czerwinski was a strict practising

All that remained of the railway junction and industrial town of Kirishi.

Catholic. I had been raised as a Catholic from birth, but not strictly, and I was certainly not a practising Catholic now. I was also not uninterested in the fair sex, but naturally not so devoted to them as the *Feldwebel* was. I had to take care! The *Unterarzt* went on: 'You must carry out conscientiously everything I tell you, then nothing can go awry. And another thing. You will stay with me to the end, I have received the agreement of Hauptmann Baldauf. But you have to take the lightning-flash badge from your sleeve. I cannot hold on to you if you don't because they are desperate for trained

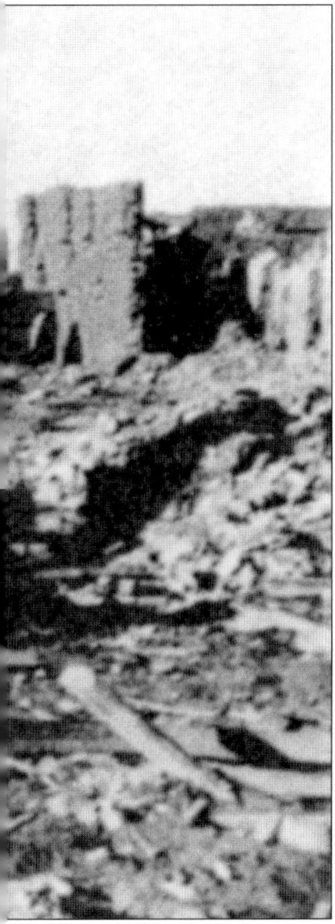

signals staff, particularly telegraphists.' I agreed and with a spark of sadness removed the lightning-flash badge.

Now I could be introduced to the patients as their new 'chief'. Every patient, whether officer or other rank, had to obey my instructions, for here in the infirmary they were patients and nothing else. Thus I was the most influential man after the doctor. The *Spiess* (RSM) with his great loud snout – I cannot call it anything else – ordered me to report on the morrow to the GvH Company (Homeland Garrison) for fresh orders. Dr Czerwinski: 'You are not going. Your place is with the sick. If he insists, I shall write him up as fit for the front. And I shall also enquire why this healthy man is still here.' From now on the *Spiess* was painstakingly considerate towards me and even sent me cigarettes.

A reinforcement arrived, a nursing sister who was about as much a nurse as I was a trained medical orderly. I shall call her Frau Helga. She was about twenty-five, tall and slim with long, dark flowing hair, warm brown eyes, soft and modest, and yet had a friendly winning way. She was the wife of a junior lieutenant working as an engineer in an important local war factory. At this time women could only remain in the locality if they were doing important war work. Therefore Frau Helga was a 'nursing sister'. With Fritz John as orderly and boilerman/porter our team was now complete. I had to be on call around the clock but I was grateful for the interesting tasks which came my way.

One evening three Ukrainian SS men were brought in with methyl alcohol poisoning. They were treated with litres of coffee

Men of 162nd Grenadier Regiment on the way to the most advanced forward positions at Chudovo in the Grusino bridgehead.

and a tube inserted to make them vomit in order to lessen the effects of the poison. It did not work; one died the same evening, the other two survived but lost their eyesight. Help also came too late to save a fifteen-year old-suicide who had gassed himself. On another occasion I had to watch the doctor lay out a tapeworm he had recovered from a patient. It had to be confirmed that the worm's head was present otherwise the whole procedure would have been in vain. Next I assisted Dr Czerwinski at the morgue for the autopsy of a field gendarme who had been murdered by a deserter. The cause of death had to be determined for the court martial. In recognition of this service the doctor gave me his alcohol and cigarette ration. He neither smoked nor drank, so this was another advantage for me since at that time I did both.

We two had become good friends without the correct gulf between the ranks having suffered. Only once did a small misunderstanding disturb our good relationship. We had agreed to meet on Easter Sunday in the Catholic Church. On the way there I discovered that Freiburg had two churches, a fact which I had not bothered to notice before, not being a church-goer. Having a closer look at the upperworks of each I saw that one had a golden cockerel, just like the Evangelical church at Dux in the Sudetenland. Therefore I went into the other church. I noticed that in this other church the baroque angels were absent, that it had windows allowing much light to enter and also some numbers on a board on the wall the purpose of which I did not understand. It was not until the whole congregation began to sing that I realised I was amongst Protestants. In Catholic churches at home we had a church choir and the only people who sang were those permitted to do so. The Protestants had the same bible and the same God but Dr Czerwinski was very reproachful. Finally he forgave my sin.

It was the end of April 1945. The Soviets and Americans had met at the Elbe so that it was now high time to think about how we would get home. Dr Czerwinski and I were agreed that we should pass through my home village and slaughter a pig to

A wrecked T-34 tank immediately before the German positions in the '*Schädeltal*' (skull valley), Kirishi bridgehead.

celebrate our having survived the war – we optimists. We had no idea that by now my parents had already been driven out of house and home. The Czech Soucek mentioned earlier had taken up occupation there and made things clear to them in the first five minutes. He had beaten up my parents, called them German swine and my mother a whore. Beneš had declared the Sudeten Germans outlaws. My former teacher had slit his wrists and other inhabitants of the village were murdered and the women raped. Our Polish housemaid did not understand it at all. She had removed my father's wallet containing 4,000 *Reichsmarks* from the writing table to a place under the floorboards so that he would have money to get by. My parents had taken refuge temporarily at my sister's house while the so-called 'partisans' from the interior of Bohemia martyred the Sudeten Germans with murder, rape and other forms of intimidation. Nowadays everybody is supposed to forgive and forget all atrocities except those committed by Germans. Sworn statements made by the victims of torture were collected by an American priest of Bohemian origin, Emmanuel Reichenberger, in his book *Europa in Trümmern*, providing appalling examples of where fanatical nationalism can lead.

In Freiburg our immediate concern was how we could become motorised having regard to the final collapse expected any day. The *Unterarzt* and I simply requisitioned whatever we needed, possibly the doctor had been given full authority to do this by the Kommandantur. First we set up a reserve dressing station in suitable cellars below a massive house at the western end of the locality, equipped it with stretchers, bandaging materials, narcotics and diverse medicaments and then went in search of suitable trucks. We found two old specimens still in good running order. Our vehicles were all painted with Red Crosses, we made armbands for ourselves and a Red Cross bonnet for Sister Helga. This was all done mainly for our peace of mind for we knew that the Russians considered the wounded still to be combatants and therefore legitimate targets for attack. We needed two ambulance drivers: two lightly wounded patients volunteered. Our small convoy of ambulances was now in service, and except for the sciatica sufferer everybody could walk, and later even he found the strength to do so when the need arose.

It was early May when we received orders to attach ourselves to 208th Division which would attempt to reach the Americans south of Prague. At that time we were not aware that it was already too late to realise the objective, for the Russians had completed a large pincer movement from Dresden and Vienna to encircle the troops inside it. In any case, even if we had reached the Americans, they were keeping to their agreement to turn over to the Russians all German troops who had been facing the Russians in the final months of the war. That was therefore the situation in Freiburg when we removed from the poster columns the photographic images of German women being raped by gloating Red Army soldiers. This was done in the interests of the members of the civilian population who had decided to remain.

We loaded supplies into our trucks. Frau Helga's husband joined us wearing his lieutenant's uniform. Fortunately we had been able to resolve the question of fuel by requisitioning thousands of litres of petrol from a filling station. The vehicles and every canister we could find were topped up to the brim. Our Freiburg battle group also acquired some girls who believed they would be safer with us.

On 7 May our convoy set off, leaving the Glatz mountains in the finest spring weather. The road to Landshut via Waldenburg was constantly uphill. Our two trucks began to boil, forcing us to stop. After a few more kilometres one of the two old trucks gave up the ghost and so we headed downhill over the Weckelsdorfer Felsen, a well-known beauty spot, into Bohemia. Trautenau was a ghost town, only Wehrmacht columns were to be seen in its narrow streets. Somewhere between Trautenau and Königgratz we followed a field path and spent the night in the open. To eat we had bread, tins of fatty meat and cheese.

On 8 May it was cooler and the roads were now blocked with German military traffic, which effectively brought our progress to an end. Our senior officer assembled us around him to announce that he had received information by radio to the effect that the war was over and the German Wehrmacht no longer had authority to issue orders. Everybody was now released from his oath of allegiance, but whoever felt safer with the unit was welcome to remain. We retained our weapons because sooner or later we expected to have to defend ourselves against Czech partisans.

On the road we met the first Czech regular police. They adopted a correct bearing and indicated that we should proceed to the collection camp at Königgratz. I had lost contact with Dr Czerwinski, Frau Helga and her husband; I directed Fritz John and our two ambulance drivers to veer away from Königgratz and eventually we joined a convoy of German trucks led by a vehicle with a mounted machine gun ready to fire. The intention was to attempt the breakthrough. When night fell the convoy snaked along narrow country lanes between Czech villages. Nobody was about, not even watching from behind their curtains. East of Pardubitz, two armed boys stopped the leading truck at a village entrance and defied us to pass. Thank heaven nobody started shooting. The mothers of the two boys appeared, imploring their sons to stop being stupid and give way, which they did and so we drove on. It would certainly have meant our deaths if the machine-gun crew had not kept their nerve.

Towards 0900 hrs on 9 or 10 May, I cannot be sure which, we came to the conclusion that our attempts to flee had no prospect of success. The Russians were already in Prague. We stopped on the highway and destroyed our weapons. To our left and right on the road were heaps of abandoned Wehrmacht equipment; fairly new banknotes of all denominations lay strewn around in masses, apparently from the regimental strong boxes. Now that we were unarmed, gendarmes and 'partisans' who appeared from their hideouts led us into a field, collected up every man's *Soldbuch* [pay/ID book] and demanded on pain of death that we hand over all ammunition. Decorations and badges of rank were also taken. Two Russians arrived, each holding aloft in one hand ten to fifteen watches and calling '*Uri, uri, uri!*' They gathered them up industriously and now had gifts for all their numerous relations.

We were made to walk in loose order, not marched, into Chrudim where old ladies of the town spat on the footpath in front of us and forced us to walk in the gutter. It was here that I saw for the last time Frau Helga and her husband; she looked frightened, while he tried to shoulder the humiliation with dignity. Old veteran soldiers – one could recognise them by the discoloured patches where their decorations and badges had been worn – and staff officers long in the tooth came in for the mockery and hatred of the rabble. Many would never forget the humiliation they had to endure, and no doubt many regretted not having taken the easy way out earlier.

CHAPTER 15

Prisoner of the Soviets

RUSSIAN TROOPS ENTERED THE TOWN. Well-nourished and well-clad young soldiers stood on the running boards of the vehicles acknowledging the welcome of the Czechs and hardly noticed us. We were stopped near a Russian horse-drawn supply unit. Some uniformed Russian girls beamed at us and shouted out, '*Voyna kaput, domoy poyecheli*,' approximately 'The war is over, you will be going home.' In between their calls a soldier with prominent cheekbones and a ferocious expression shouted the hate-filled sentence, 'You will all go to Siberia and work until you shit blood.' This made the girls indignant and they rebuked him before turning to us and calling, 'No, no, don't believe him, you're going home.' They really believed it. But the prediction of the 'angry Ivan' proved to be the correct one, and in all respects.

The football ground at Chrudim was our first camp. For three days we stayed there in the blazing May sunshine without any shade, and at night we froze. Czechs guarded us. They separated out the military police and made them dig latrines, beating them as they did so. We heard their cries of pain; now and again a shot rang out. They were at the far end of the playing field so that we did not know what went on there. A relatively small boy, aged about fourteen, who wore German uniform and spoke with a Bavarian dialect was tied by the Czechs to a goalpost. Alternately he insulted the Czechs, and the Germans who would not dare go to his aid, as 'You cowards'. Eventually he got free in the evening.

For two days we received nothing to eat, on the third day thirty-two men were given a freshly baked loaf of bread to share. At night they fired machine guns for practice just above our heads. On the second day I volunteered for a road-sweeping party simply to get out of the place.

With brooms and watering cans we set out to cleanse the dirty streets of this small town. The local population left us in peace. Apparently the difference was becoming clearer to them in many respects between a German occupation and a Russian 'liberation'. I went to fill my watering can at the public hospital. Offering me a slice of buttered bread and a glass of milk, a middle-aged woman there said to me in broken German, 'Take these, you mustn't think all Czechs are so bad.' It is always the women amongst all peoples who help overcome hate or prevent it beginning. I thanked her in textbook Czech such as we had been taught at commercial school. This woman was sad that the chapter of our common history had ended for the two peoples of Bohemia with so much spillage of German blood. The Czech guard who escorted us back after work became talkative after I told him that I originated from the Teplitz-Schönau region. 'I am guarding you here while at home the Russians make free with my wife. They say they are liberators and I should be grateful to them.' For this man the Slav brothers were not quite as he had visualised them.

The following night the sky was lit by flares and starshells and to the west the Prague area flickered brightly – victory fireworks. They were celebrating our defeat. It was said that the Waffen-SS were still resisting in the sewers. Captured SS men were broken on the wheel and quartered, or dragged by vehicles through the streets until dead. Wounded German soldiers were thrown from the top floors of military hospitals. All Germans in Prague were hunted down and killed, or petrol poured over them, set alight and made to run across the Charles Bridge as living torches. These bestialities, repeated in whispers, reduced us to helpless hatred, as much against the British and Americans who permitted it.

At night the Russians arrived, shining torches over our blankets. Since nobody had a watch any more, now they wanted our boots. If they left their own behind in the exchange then a man was in luck, but even luckier if his size didn't fit the Russian. Another group of Russians conducted a search under the blankets for women and girls being hidden there. Their pleas when caught fell on deaf ears; they were taken off and never seen again. Poor Helga!

Next afternoon we witnessed the following scene: a funeral cortège came from the town, the waggon containing the coffin being horse-drawn as is the tradition in Bohemia. From the other direction, heading into town, was a column of *panje*-waggons. The cortège was stopped, its large strong horses unharnessed and exchanged for the two small *panje* horses. Then the mourners were rounded up and robbed of anything valuable. The Russians exacted a very personal price for liberating the Czechs.

Next day the Russians took over the camp and marched us off to Leitomischl. The guards were Asiatic and behaved correctly, protecting us on the way against Czechs approaching too close. At Leitomischl we were lodged at the castle, given haircuts down to the scalp, a commission gave us a quick once-over and divided us into three groups. We were given soup in tin cans three times daily, having no mess tins. Food was mostly Wehrmacht deep-frozen green beans and spinach.

It was a punishable offence to speculate as to our possible destination. A Russian major assured me that we would be going home soon and were being registered. It was at Leitomischl that I met Dr Czerwinski again. He had been placed with the officers. Depressed he told me, '*Herr* Steiniger, there is no release, they are putting us into three workgroups. Why do you think they are cutting our hair so short?' He gave me a sad wave in parting. It was the last time I ever saw him.

Here at Leitomischl a *Volksdeutscher* asked permission to visit his Czech aunt. He was given permission and a Czech guard. When he returned he reported that the Czechs were not happy with their liberation. 'My aunt said, the Czechs were often afraid of the Germans, but they tremble in fear of the Russians.' It was rumoured that millions of Sudeten Germans in Czechoslovakia were being deported. I doubted this latrine gossip but found it difficult to imagine how Germans and Czechs could live together peaceably in future. The 'Czech-isation' was already being carried out ruthlessly, and as we know now within two generations at most there are very few Germans in Bohemia and Moravia, only a hybrid group indifferent as to whether it is classified as one or the other.

Next day we were loaded into cattle trucks and taken by train to Auschwitz. It was rumoured that there had been a large concentration camp there. We marched into it beneath an arched portal bearing the inscription '*Arbeit macht frei*'. This cynical motto would apply to us, for those who managed to survive the years of hunger in Soviet prison camps would indeed eventually find their freedom through loyal hard work in the vast wastes of Siberia and its developing industries. It would take years, however, in my case four and a half. We did not suspect a thing, for the Geneva Convention made it illegal at the end of a war for prisoners to be detained *sine die* without the possibility of release. However, we heard that at one of their conferences, the victorious powers – USSR, USA and Great Britain – had decided to abrogate the convention.

Our stay at Auschwitz lasted four days and here we were very well fed for the forthcoming journey. We were expecting to be engaged on harvest work in the Ukraine lasting for the summer, but unknown to us ahead lay a railway journey in a cattle truck which lasted six weeks until about 11 July 1945 when we were unloaded at Ossinniki on the northern slopes of the Altai mountains, 400 kilometres south-east of Novossibirsk, for slave labour.

Very much has been written about the conditions which prevailed for German prisoners in Soviet work camps in the years following the defeat. My own story might fill another book. Therefore I conclude here with an Epilogue relating how it was possible for me as a slave labourer to maintain contacts with my family and fiancée during the period of my incarceration.

Epilogue

IN THE LAST DAYS OF AUGUST 1945, my parents' farm and my sister's house were taken without compensation. My mother and father, and my sister Mimi with her two small children, were taken to the border between Bohemia and Saxony. After a final search to ensure that they had no possessions but the clothes they wore, they were pushed across the frontier into Germany with the official parting words, '*Heim ins Reich!*' I knew nothing of all this.

From the middle of 1946, we slave labourers were allowed to write one Soviet Red Cross postcard of twenty-five words every two months. I wrote to my parents at our address in the Sudetenland but received no reply.

On 8 November 1946 I wrote a postcard to my fiancée care of the Netzschkau/Vogtland post office, my last known address for her. 'In this way, I wish a Happy Christmas, to yourself and your parents and if possible to mine. Fervently awaiting reply. Heartiest greetings, Erhard.'

In May 1947 I received my first letter from her from postwar Germany. She was now living in Kiel after rediscovering her parents in Schleswig-Holstein. She had no news of my parents.

By December 1948 I was in a camp at Stalinsk. My mother, who was living in Eckartsberga in the Soviet-occupied zone of Germany, had begun searching for my fiancée, had found her and obtained my camp address. In her letter she confirmed that my brother Franz was alive and in a prison camp in the Urals.

From now on I began to receive regular mail from my mother and fiancée, and in my letter of 17 January 1949 I thanked my fiancée for her help: 'It is always the most pleasant moment of the day for me when I think of you before sleep, and try to imagine our reunion, and how we will build our new life together . . .'

At the end of August 1949 all inmates at the Stalinsk camp had to fall in with possessions to hear a brief political address, and then we were transferred to the mineworkers' camp for our discharge by goods train. By the time we got to Brest-Litovsk where we changed trains for the German eastern zone I had still not yet decided whether to give my home address as Eckartsberga or Kiel.

I asked the locomotive driver what he thought: 'If you are free and single, go to the West! Otherwise the only work you will get is at the Aue uranium mine or in the Volkspolizei.'

When my train arrived at Frankfurt/Oder on 1 October 1949, the loudspeakers warned that the address which we now had to declare was final, and we had to take the correct train to go there. I struggled with my decision for two hours. I was now twenty-nine years of age and could not hang on to my mother's apron strings for ever, however much I loved her. I certainly did not fancy uranium mining or the police. 'Where to?' the ticket clerk demanded.

'Kiel, Oldenburg-Strasse 14'. With that I had committed myself. I sent a telegram: 'Arriving Monday or Tuesday. Greetings, Erhard.'

My fiancée Els had formerly had to share a room with other girls in a barrack hut but was now renting a furnished room in Kiel. I wanted her as my wife but we had only known each other for a total of seven hours apart from our countless letters. What did I have to offer her? Her risk was immeasurably greater than mine.

'Kiel, main station. All change!' I was the last to leave the carriage and walked slowly along the platform holding a cardboard suitcase and a pack of *machorka* tobacco – my worldly possessions. The roof of the station concourse was still in ruins. My fiancée was waiting as arranged at the station's Red Cross post when she saw an unkempt 'returner-home' with a 'wild look' approaching. She stood before me at the barrier. We exchanged smiles as if we had only been apart since yesterday.

Illustration Acknowledgements

Photographs of north-west Bohemia and the Kurische Nehrung originate from the archive of Rautenberg Verlag; views of Tilsit and the Königin Luise Bridge are from Walther Hubatsch.

All other photos come from the author's collection and the following individuals:

Rittmeister (ret'd) Gerhard Baltruschat (former commander, 14th Company, 151st Grenadier Regiment)
School headmaster (ret'd) Bruno Grützmacher (former Oberleutnant, regimental staff, 151st Grenadier Regiment)
Prof. Dr Walther Hubatsch (former chief of signals, 151st Grenadier Regiment)
Oberstleutnant Wilhelm Kubel (Bundeswehr, ret'd, former Hauptmann and battalion commander, 162nd Grenadier Regiment)

I extend my grateful thanks to all of them.

The Author